SEVEN CLIMBS

FINDING THE FINEST CLIMB ON EACH CONTINENT

CHARLES SHERWOOD

Vertebrate Publishing, Sheffield
www.v-publishing.co.uk

SEVEN CLIMBS

CHARLES SHERWOOD

First published in 2020 by Vertebrate Publishing.

Vertebrate Publishing
Omega Court, 352 Cemetery Road, Sheffield S11 8FT, United Kingdom.
www.v-publishing.co.uk

Cover: the author on the Spenceley Glacier, South Georgia. Photo: Stephen Reid.
Photography by Charles Sherwood unless otherwise credited.
Illustrations copyright © Andy Kirkpatrick 2020.
Extract from *The Waste Land* by T.S. Eliot reproduced by permission of Faber and Faber Ltd.

This book is a work of non-fiction based on the life and experiences of Charles Sherwood. The author has stated to the publishers that, except in such minor respects not affecting the substantial accuracy of the work, the contents of the book are true.

A CIP catalogue record for this book is available from the British Library.

ISBN: 978-1-912560-85-1 (Paperback)
ISBN: 978-1-912560-86-8 (Ebook)

10 9 8 7 6 5 4 3 2 1

Every effort has been made to obtain the necessary permissions with reference to copyright material, both illustrative and quoted. We apologise for any omissions in this respect and will be pleased to make the appropriate acknowledgements in any future edition.

Cover design by Jane Beagley, typesetting by Cameron Bonser, Vertebrate Publishing.

Vertebrate Publishing is committed to printing on paper from sustainable sources.

Printed and bound in the UK by T.J. International Ltd, Padstow, Cornwall.

For
Rosemary & the 3 Ts

With special thanks to those mountain guides and other
professional climbers prepared to tie on to the same rope
as someone so much less experienced than themselves:

*Bruno Richard, Mark Seaton, Bob Barton, Adrian Ballinger,
Brian Warren, Chad Peele, Dorje Sherpa, Kharma Sherpa,
Aaron Jones, Andy Kirkpatrick, Jaime Avila, Eric Ostopkevich,
Dean Staples, Stephen Venables & Skip Novak*

CONTENTS

THE CHALLENGE

The sun went down at precisely 8.05 p.m., leaving me with just the light of my headlamp. The rope snaked above me into the unknown as I teetered on the tips of my twin axes and the front points of my crampons. I was on the Second Ice Field of the Eigerwand or, to use its English name, the North Face of the Eiger. Climbing this route in the dark might have seemed foolhardy – most especially when lacking any great skill as a mountaineer – but things were OK. The ice was in good condition: soft enough to penetrate with a single swing of the axe, yet firm enough to bear a man's weight. In short, perfect *névé*. And although the natural light had gone, the ice adequately reflected the beam from my headlamp, easing progress.

Then everything became un-OK. The Second Ice Field is prone to icefall and rockfall, and just then it started to fall apart. There was a flurry above and a large chunk of ice and rock broke free and fell through the dark on to my head. I could do nothing but cling to my tenuous position, resisting the temptation to look up as the debris hurtled over me. One piece gashed my nose. Rather more concerning, another shattered my headlamp. I was now in true darkness.

Such a situation tends to prompt two big questions (intermingled with suitable expletives): what am I doing here? And what am I going to do now? Both occurred in rapid succession, including the expletives. However, I remained essentially calm. The alternative did not appear promising.

The first priority was to try to rescue the headlamp, since I had no spare. Fortunately, the ice was so steep, and my body so pressed against it, that the broken pieces, rather than disappearing into the void below, had wedged themselves between my chest and the slope. I collected all those I could find and tucked them into a pocket. Trying to reassemble them there and then was out of the question, but at least there was the hope of getting the headlamp working again later.

Second, I dug out my small radio and contacted Mark, my partner and guide, who I very much hoped was securely belayed somewhere above me (although we hadn't seen many secure belays thus far). I explained the situation, then up I went. Technical climbing in the pitch dark can be challenging, especially when it's on the North Face of the Eiger, but at least ice is better than rock. It's more uniform. In such circumstances, the best strategy follows the proverb about how to eat an elephant: one bite at a time. Just keep making steady progress. I did, feeling my way with each placement. Always three points of contact, moving just one limb at a time. It felt a long and lonely climb, but eventually Mark and I were reunited. And – serendipitously – the headlamp was repairable, and light was restored.

It took us four days to scale that face and get down the other side. But rather than being the end of a journey, it proved to be the beginning of one. An idea had taken root.

Two decades earlier a pair of American businessmen, Dick Bass and Frank Wells, had set themselves the task of climbing the highest summit on each of the seven continents. It was an inspiring project and one recorded in their enthralling book, *Seven Summits*. Many others since have taken up the challenge. There is even a commercial organisation of the same name dedicated to helping climbers achieve this goal. Such is the popularity of the Seven Summits that these seven 'easiest' routes to the top of each continent are now among the busiest climbing venues in the world. They offer many things, but wilderness is no longer one of them. The encampment at the bottom of Everest and the infamous queues on the mountain's summit ridge are just the best-known illustrations of what has happened.

By contrast, a notable feature of our climb on the North Face was the solitude. In those four days, we had not seen a single other person. The mountain has a mystique unrivalled in Europe, because of its aesthetics and its history – the drama played out on its dark, forbidding face. And yet, its technical difficulty means that it is still climbed infrequently compared with the popular routes on other high-profile Alpine peaks such as Mont Blanc and the Matterhorn.

That got me thinking. Could I find similar challenges elsewhere? 'Seven Summits' that represented not the highest, but the finest of mountaineering objectives on each of the seven continents – in short, the best seven climbs in the world? Such a selection would need to reflect mountaineering challenge, natural beauty and historical context; and to capture something of both the diverse character of each continent and the sheer variety of climbing in all its forms. The choice would of course be highly subjective and hugely contentious. But all the better for that. After all, independently spirited mountaineers enjoy little more than a hearty argument.

And so began a personal quest …

North Face of the Eiger.

EUROPE

Climbing for me really began at university. After a faltering start, my academic performance had improved considerably – a function of studiousness rather than any real talent – and I found myself with a scholarship to Cambridge University. Cambridge is in the Fens, famous for being flat, wet and windy. There is nothing to climb. Well, not quite nothing.

These days, I'm told, Cambridge is a demanding institution. But back in the late 1970s it was almost impossible to fail. There was only one thing you could do that meant automatic expulsion, and that was climbing on the college buildings. This of course made the idea irresistible. A lifetime's friendship was created as I teamed up with a fellow fresher, Bill Medlicott, who had not only undertaken an entire week's introductory climbing course in North Wales but was also the proud owner of a rope. In our inaugural term, we put up a bold first ascent of the South-West Ridge of Sidney Sussex Chapel – at least, it was bold if you'd barely climbed before. I recall standing on the chapel roof, about to abseil down the rope now dangling into the courtyard below, when a college porter strode by. I thought, 'If he looks up, that's it. We won't have made even one term.' Mercifully he didn't.

Other antics followed. A papier-mâché Easter rabbit found its way up to the college bell tower, and a park bench up on to the rear gate of King's. All this high-spirited fun came to a climax when a plan was hatched to put our sixteenth-century college up for sale. We duly gathered from around town all the estate agents' For Sale signs we could find. These – hereinafter known as 'the stolen property' – were suitably adapted and, during the night, hung out on the college walls. A harmless prank, of course … but not in the eyes of Police Constable Ron Pearce. This fearless bastion of law and order cornered various student members on a narrow staircase and called for backup. Bill was one of those packed into a Black Maria and taken away to spend the night at Her Majesty's pleasure in one of the local cells. Fortunately, he was able to secure a timely release in the morning on the entirely truthful grounds that, as a theology student, he was also sacristan of the college chapel (the same one we had previously climbed) and needed to prepare for Holy Communion. His prompt release was particularly welcome, because that day he was receiving a visit from his parents, his father being the then president of the Kent Law Society. Happily, the president took these developments in his judicial stride.

Meanwhile, our focus had shifted to real rock, and excursions to the Peak District, North Wales and the Lakes. As a kid who had spent most of his summers on bucket-and-spade holidays abroad, my eyes were opened for the first time to the beauty of my own country. The climbing was self-taught, Bill and I guiding each other as we alternated places at the 'sharp end' of the rope. It was a good early test of nerve, because while cams (modern devices to protect against a fall) had been invented, we could afford only one prototype between us. Our main protection was still the legendary 'chock' or 'nut', the MOAC Original: very effective when suitable cracks in the rock were available, but no use at all when they weren't.

Then life got serious. I took up a high-pressure job and thought myself very important. I decamped to the USA for a couple of years to do an

MBA and returned to an even higher-pressure job, persuaded that I was now even more important. Bill and I married (different women, not each other) and children followed. We continued to climb, but it was distinctly sporadic. We weren't exactly at the cutting edge, or any other kind of edge. Indeed, at the crag, fellow climbers would sometimes gaze at us and our dated gear as though we were exhibits in a quaint folk museum. But we did keep going in one fashion or another.

In the summer of 1992, my wife Rosemary and I had just taken on a new home and were expecting our second child. I thought this would be the ideal moment for my first climbing trip to the Alps. Needless to say, Rosemary was 'delighted'. I took on a French guide, Bruno Richard, with whom I had previously skied. He was known among my friends as Mad Bruno, but for home consumption I rebranded him Bruno the Wary. Rosemary was not fooled. Nonetheless, Bruno and I headed for Zermatt in the Valais. In a single week, we climbed the Breithorn and Castor, traversed the Liskamm and the Monte Rosa, and finished up with the Matterhorn and the Dom. This packed itinerary was made possible by extraordinarily good weather. I came away thinking this was what climbing in the Alps was always like. Many dark days since, cowering from rain and wind in Chamonix, have corrected all such delusions.

The following spring, Bruno introduced me to ski touring. Gentle introductions were not Bruno's big thing; nor was acclimatisation. He felt that a great way to have a first go at ski touring would be to climb Mont Blanc on skis. So, having flown in from London the day before, I joined him for the long skin up to the Grands Mulets Hut. From there we ascended at 2 a.m. the following day, our touring skis on our backs, to reach the highest summit in the Alps. With the world now beneath us, we stepped again into those skis and for the first time I used them in downhill mode, straight off the top. We descended the North Face – which sounds rather daring, but it's actually the mountain's gentlest side. Gentle or not, by the time I reached the mid-station of the Aiguille du Midi cable car

I was hyperventilating so badly that my fellow passengers clearly thought I was about to die – and I wasn't sure they were mistaken.

Within a few weeks, Bruno was in hospital, having fallen through a snow bridge into a crevasse. He had been an inspiring guide and had my true sympathy, but I did feel there was a message here and, with thoughts of my continued survival high in my mind, I reluctantly drew a close to our climbing partnership.

With each ending there is a new beginning. I was introduced by an older and wiser friend to a new guide, an Englishman a few years younger than I was, who had moved with his fiancée to Chamonix. Mark Seaton has lived there ever since, and with Jane has brought up three daughters, all extraordinarily good skiers. His parental duties inspired his other profession, that of children's author. He created *Mark the Mountain Guide*.

Mark was a young guide with considerable climbing ambition. But that ambition included becoming an old guide. A Mancunian who had done much of his mountaineering in Scotland, he bore that sense of caution that came from repeated exposure to the unpredictable conditions in the UK's 'frozen north'. I sometimes moaned that he could interpret almost any weather forecast as bad. A degree of caution, though, seemed a sensible counterbalance to my own tendency to 'go for it, come what may'. And out of our climbing partnership was to be forged something deeper still: a lifelong friendship.

Mark brought with him a new concept: the route. The focus of my very limited alpine climbing to this point had been getting to the top of things – the bigger the better, but always by the easiest route. Mark had this idea that you could make things more interesting (Rosemary would say 'even more pointless') if you chose a harder route to the top. New itineraries now emerged such as the North Face of the Tour Ronde, the Forbes Arête on the Chardonnet, the Traverse of the Grands Charmoz and Grépon, the Biancograt on Piz Bernina, the North-East Face of Piz

Badile, and the Frendo Spur and Rébuffat routes, both on the Aiguille du Midi. Getting to the top by the route of least resistance was now saved largely for ski touring: snowy peaks such as the Dômes de Miage in France, the Gran Paradiso in Italy and the Nordend on the Swiss Monte Rosa, the latter undertaken as a finale to the popular Haute Route between Chamonix and Zermatt. There were adventures and happy memories to go with them all, but as we did these many varied climbs, we thought always of just one. Mark and I shared a gnawing obsession: to climb the North Face of the Eiger.

Quite why we were so obsessed with the Eiger's North Face, I do not know. Mark had attempted it many times – always with other guides – and failed on each occasion. But, as a reason for trying again, that's about as rational as banging your head against a wall. As an ex-history student, I was fascinated by the tortured narrative of the first climbs on the Face – the initial setbacks and ultimate success in the years running up to the Second World War. However, reading a library full of books about it was one thing, climbing it was another. Nor were we drawn by its appearance. The Face cannot really be described as beautiful. It does not smile. Sometimes it just broods; generally, it scowls. It is threatening, not welcoming. So why? Why were we so obsessed? There is an aura. That is all I can say.

My first trip to the Bernese Oberland, home of the Eiger, was in 1996. The mountain railway, the Jungfraubahn, whisked Mark and me up high on to the snowy plateau, allowing relatively easy ascents of the Mönch and the Jungfrau. We were determined, though, to do the Eiger properly, rather than simply wander up its comparatively easy West Flank. We waited for a strong weather forecast and ascended the famous Mittellegi Ridge, with its precipitous views on the right down the North Face. The gnawing obsession only gnawed harder.

It wasn't until 2005 that I stepped for the first time on to the North Face itself. It was only a reconnaissance. Mark had been on the lower face many times before, but he wanted to remind himself of the part of the

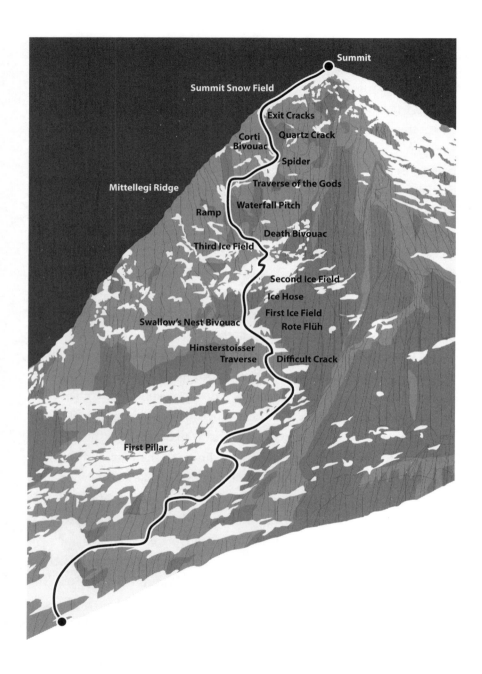

route that we would need to complete in the early hours before dawn – that is, in the dark.

We climbed to the top of the Difficult Crack, which proved to be just that. This is the first real challenge on the Face and its name elegantly understates the grunting, shuffling indignities required to overcome it. Mark led the way up and over this obstacle without his pack, leaving me to follow with the baggage. Inelegant as we were, we made it in reasonable form. But without crampons or other equipment, we could go no further. We turned back, abseiling down the route we'd come up. Sadly, plans to mount a full assault two days later were left in shreds by that great shredder of all alpine ambition, the weather. It snowed, and I returned to work.

We were back, though, in October of the following year with a vengeance and a strong weather forecast. This time we were fully equipped, loaded with heavy packs. Once more we struggled up the Difficult Crack, me again in the role of laden mule. Things looked good. And then it started to snow. And it didn't stop. This wasn't part of the plan at all. The sense of drama was heightened by the sound of a rotor blade overhead. The rescue helicopter was out: elsewhere on the mountain, another party or parties were in trouble.

Meanwhile, a long traverse to our left proved much more testing than we had anticipated. Not only was fresh snow falling, but the stuff that had fallen above was pouring down the Face in great flurries – in effect mini avalanches. Mark now had to climb into this, flailing with his axes at the unconsolidated snow and often doing no more than raking it back down on top of him. Eventually, though, he established himself in a stance on the cliffs above me, and I was able to follow.

I arrived about twenty minutes later in what felt like a blizzard: snow apparently coming from every direction, whipped up by a strong wind. We were on steep ground and, with me slightly below Mark, my head was roughly level with his waist. That meant quite a shock when I turned to look at him, because right in front of my eyes was an exposed set of male genitalia! The simple explanation was that Mark had arrived at the top of the pitch and secured his belay. Desperate for a pee, he had embarked on the task, only to be caught mid-process by a massive spindrift avalanche that had filled his jacket and trousers with snow and spun him upside down, leaving him winded and disorientated. He had managed to right himself, but, in the excitement, had overlooked the all-important action of restoring the tackle to its proper place. Woe betide him!

This information came later. At that moment all I could think of was how to alert Mark to the situation. Englishmen are characteristically awkward about discussing genitalia and related subjects and tend to revert to more or less obscure euphemisms. This, combined with the howling gale around us, led to a somewhat surreal exchange, bellowed at full volume along the following lines:

Author: 'Mark, you're all exposed.'
Mark: 'I know we're exposed. It's a blizzard!'
Author: 'But, Mark, you're hanging out!'
Mark: 'Of course I'm hanging on. What else do you expect?'
Author: 'You're undone!'
Mark: 'Yes, we're done. We've got to get out of here.'

In the end there was nothing for it but to point directly at the object(s) in question, now a worryingly frosty white. Realising what had happened, a look of horror transformed Mark's face. The frozen appendage was hastily tucked away, but not without much apprehension as to how much damage had already been done.

What to do now? One thing was clear. We couldn't stay where we were. It was already late in the day and the priority was to find a safe (or safe-ish) place for the night. This wasn't it, because apart from there being nowhere to sit down, let alone lay out a sleeping bag, we were badly exposed to avalanche from above.

We had now reached the beginning of a traverse famous, or perhaps more accurately infamous, among climbers. In 1936 Anderl Hinterstoisser led the second-ever attempt on the Face. At this point he succeeded in crossing the bare limestone, polished smooth by rockfall. His three partners followed. Then, fatally, they took back in the rope after them, cutting off their retreat. A storm blew up, Hinterstoisser himself fell, and each of his comrades died in turn, leaving only the desperate young guide, Toni Kurz, fighting for survival. His final words, 'I'm finished', uttered almost within reach of rescue, have resounded ever since through the annals of mountaineering history.

For us there was good news and bad news. The good news was that there was a fixed rope in place across the traverse. The bad news was that the traverse was not dry rock, but sheet ice. However, we had a strong motivation. We knew that if we could only get to the other side, we would find a ledge, small but overhung and therefore beautifully protected: the Swallow's Nest bivouac.

That left just the little matter of getting across. Mark strapped his pack back on and set off along the fixed rope, with me belaying him from behind. Too late, I realised I was still wearing my lightweight gloves rather than the double gloves buried deep in my pack. Soon Mark became just a vague shadow in the driving snow. Then he disappeared altogether. Finally, darkness fell. It took a long, long time. My cold hands started to lose sensation. I had rarely felt so alone. There were strange tugs and gyrations on the rope, but I couldn't really fathom what was happening. I just gradually paid out the rope, as I judged it was needed. I learnt later that Mark had fallen, and though he had been caught by the fixed rope, he was turned upside down and pinned in that position by the weight of his heavy pack. He had only barely been able to extricate himself.

Hours passed, or so it seemed. At last there was a call on the radio. Mark had made it to the bivouac. I followed, fully appreciating the challenge he had overcome, as I now faced the same. Even with crampons, it was near impossible to get a purchase on the ice. It was also impossible to rely entirely on the fixed rope. The anchor points were too infrequent, meaning that between each one I sank down, making it very tricky to get back up the icy rope to reach the next one. By the time I made the bivouac, I was exhausted.

But we were safe. At least for now. Meanwhile, the helicopter had been active. We later learnt that it had pulled two other groups off the Face, both having fallen before they could reach a bivouac. It now visited our small ledge, hovering opposite us in the darkness with its bright searchlight. The pilot and his team were clearly keen to know what condition we were in. Mark and I each raised a single arm to signal that we were OK, and the helicopter returned to base.

In his book *The Beckoning Silence*, Joe Simpson described how his own attempt on the Eigerwand ended at this bivouac. He and his partner were also caught here in a storm. As they huddled together, they were shocked to see two other climbers, Matthew Hayes and Philip O'Sullivan, fall from the Second Ice Field above, past their overhung shelter and down – precipitously down – to the rocks below. Simpson commented: 'We didn't hear them go. They didn't scream.'[1] He and his partner understandably decided to call it a day.

The Swallow's Nest bivouac is the size of a large ironing board. This seemed a rather small bedroom to me at the time. I have since learnt that, as bivouacs go, it's at the luxury end of things. We got out our sleeping bags, brewed up, ate some food, and generally had a pretty good night.

The morning, though, presented two distinct problems. The first was the state of our little hill. There was uncompacted snow everywhere, with much of it pouring down the Face in a relentless 'waterfall'. Even my rampant optimism couldn't brush this one off. The Face would be unclimbable for many days. There was no prospect of continuing upwards. That left the obvious alternative of retreat. But this too looked dangerous. And then there was the little matter of the frozen piece of anatomy.

Mark looked at me sheepishly and said he needed a second opinion. Dutifully I clambered over to him on all fours and peered at his groin. The things one does for one's *Bergführer*! It was not a pretty sight. When soft tissue of this kind is even lightly damaged, it tends to swell up to monstrous proportions and turn an angry scarlet. This was no exception. There was definitely evidence of frostbite, or at least frostnip. My optimistic 'I think it'll be fine' fell rather flat in the face of such visible distortions. Mark, understandably enough, was keen to have his appendage properly cared for. He picked up his mobile phone and called for the helicopter. His conversation with the rescue dispatcher, explaining the nature of his injury, must go down as, to use his own words, 'the most bizarre request for rescue in the whole history of the North Face of the Eiger.' But in other respects the phone call was rather mundane, as though one was calling for a local taxi.

Having said that, this taxi ride was more memorable than most. The helicopter hovered in front of us for a reconnaissance, returned to base for some extended planning and then joined us once more opposite our bivouac. The overhung nature of the Swallow's Nest now created an additional obstacle. The rescue guide had to be lowered on a long line and swung into us. A delicate operation, but one that the Swiss team executed flawlessly. The guide grabbed me on an incoming swing and secured me to himself with a harness. I released myself from my anchors and together we swung out into the void, enjoying what must rate as one of the finest possible views of the North Face. As we drew away, I took in the chilling insignificance of our tiny perch, clinging to an apparently vertical face, with snow cascading down it on all sides.

This particular taxi ride didn't actually involve getting into the taxi. Instead, the helicopter simply lowered me on the line on to the pastures of Alpiglen. There waiting was the rescue manager, his team, and of course a paramedic. And what a paramedic! She was perhaps mid-twenties and undeniably attractive. Was my partner hurt, she asked. 'Well, yes,'

I said. 'Mild frostbite,' I added, barely disguising a schoolboy smirk. Mark arrived shortly and the paramedic offered him two options. Either he could go directly by helicopter to the hospital in Interlaken or, if he preferred, she could first undertake a preliminary examination. Mark was very clear in his choice: Interlaken!

I collected Mark from the hospital just a few hours later. Happily, everything was in working order. Our attempt on the Face was dead and done for another year, but at least we remained intact.

You might think that by this stage it was time to find some other challenge. But neither Mark nor I had that much imagination. We had fixed this climb in our minds, and that was it. Of course, we took on other climbs, but we always had half an eye on the latest Swiss weather forecast. It was at the top of an ice climb in Chamonix the following September (2007) that Mark showed me the five-day forecast for the Bernese Oberland: an unbroken series of radiant sun symbols. There was little discussion. We abseiled off, packed our stuff into his Land Rover Defender and headed straight for the Eiger.

We checked into the little hostel close to the tunnel entrance of the Jungfraubahn, the railway that climbs beneath the Eiger and Jungfrau and disgorges tourists and others on to the plateau above. By this stage, we had twice done the tedious scrambling up the lower reaches of the Eiger and had no desire to go through all that again. So, we had devised something of a cheat. We would use the early hours of darkness to walk up the tunnel and emerge on to the North Face beyond the worst part of the scrambling, but well before the first real climbing. The tunnel is single track and barely wider than the locomotive and carriages that use it, so I made a careful study of the railway timetable to ensure that there would be no trains at that time.

We left the hotel at 4.30 a.m. and soon reached the tunnel entrance. In we went. With a handrail as aid and our headlamps for light, progress was easy and perfectly pleasant … until there was a noise, almost indiscernible at first but getting louder. Then a faint glow ahead, which became a light. It was 5 a.m. What was a train doing coming down the mountain at 5 a.m.? The service certainly wasn't listed on the public timetable. All of a sudden, speculative explanations seemed much less important than hard facts. There is no passing room on the track, and we were about to be run over by a train, a somewhat ignominious end to our not-yet-hour-long attempt on the Eigerwand.

Mark and I turned tail and raced back down the track. We moved as fast as we could, conscious though that a trip might be (embarrassingly) fatal. With seconds to spare, we found a tiny alcove and forced ourselves in. The train was upon us and Mark just had a moment to yell 'Headlamp!' I switched mine off and we prayed the driver hadn't seen us. The train ground to a halt; a guard got out at the rear and peered into the darkness, searching the tunnel with his torch, before finally resuming his journey. Did he see us? I don't know.

The rest of the walk up the tunnel was rather less relaxed as a result, but at 5.30 we at last reached the Stollenloch entrance, which allows access to the lower reaches of the Eigerwand. There we ate an orange – our last fresh anything for a while – adjusted kit and ventured out. It was not a hospitable place. There was a great deal of snow at our feet and above us loomed steep rock plastered with ice. It had a dark, wintry feel. Mark admitted to feeling depressed. The whole thing did not look promising.

But, as so often happens, our spirits rose with the dawn. We needed further encouragement, though, and hoped we might have found some in the form of a thick fixed rope going up from the tunnel entrance. Where did the rope go? Would it take us to the Hinterstoisser (good!) or to some dead-end under the huge precipice of the Rote Flüh (bad!)? It turned out neither. The rope did take us, with some considerable exertion, to the Rote Flüh, but a relatively easy traverse allowed us to get across from there to a position beneath our old favourite, the Difficult Crack. Although we had probably gained nothing, we had lost little.

This was the third time Mark and I had taken on the Crack, and we did it in time-honoured fashion. He removed his pack and then climbed on one rope, leaving the other as a haul line. With limited 'tat' (old gear left by previous parties) to pull on and lots of ice, it wasn't easy. Indeed, at one stage the only purchase Mark could get was through backwards leveraging on an under-cut hold with the point of his axe, but he made it. I followed, heaving up my own sack as I climbed on one rope, while pushing Mark's ahead of me as he hauled it up on the other.

The pitches over to the Hinterstoisser Traverse were unexpectedly demanding, although this time on rock rather than ice and *névé*. Without the storm of the previous year swirling around us, the Traverse itself was much less difficult. It was badly iced, but there were strong fixed ropes in place, and I got myself across fairly easily using a combination of Tyrolean traverse (essentially sliding along the fixed rope) and a lot of pulling. This time Mark didn't fall, and we reached the Swallow's Nest bivouac without incident.

The bivouac looked different from when we had slept there the previous October. There was much less snow now, which made it seem larger but less flat. From here we could still retreat easily; beyond here any retreat would in all likelihood have to be via (another) rescue. As Mark put it, we would no longer be cragging on the Eiger. It still wasn't even 3 p.m. and we had a full five hours of light left. We had a choice: sit it out in the bivouac or try to get to the next one, but in the knowledge that we might not reach that far by nightfall. I thought it an easy decision and said so. We could not squander five hours of light. We must push on.

The weather overhead was holding well, but the conditions underfoot were not easy. The Eigerwand can appear very different depending on which way you're looking at it. Gazing up, the climber sees only the vertical or overhanging surfaces, which tend not to hold the snow and thus give the appearance of dry rock. But gazing down, the eye discovers the thin horizontal ledges, filled with snow and ice and creating a distinctly wintry scene. All too often, that deposit of snow and ice melts a little during the day, coating the rock with dripping water that refreezes at night to create verglas, a veneer of translucent ice too thin to hold an axe or crampon, but more than slippery enough to rebuff the untooled hand or foot. These were very much the conditions we experienced. In such circumstances, crampons were essential and yet often frustratingly ineffective.

We started with a slightly awkward descent left from the Swallow's Nest, but soon established ourselves on good ice on the First Ice Field. This, though, fairly quickly ran thin as rock and ice became treacherously mixed in the area generally referred to as the Ice Hose. This was the toughest climbing we had faced so far. People tend to associate extreme climbing with pure rock or virgin ice. But, as in the case of verglas, it's often the combination of the two that is the most troublesome: thin ice over rock. Mark was pushed by this vertiginous skating rink on to the rocks ever further left, and was soon staring back at a long, long runout. He searched for some kind of spike or other protuberance to place a sling over; or for a crack into which he might insert a nut or cam. A karabiner attached to either of these would have allowed him to feed the rope he trailed through it and thus reduce the extent of any fall. But neither was available. He moved on and the runout just got longer. If he were to slip now, he would go a long way before I could arrest his fall. It would certainly test our belay anchors. Mark searched again for some way to protect himself. At last he found a placement for a cam and, using a tension traverse off this, he forced a big move back right and, to his evident relief, found more secure ground.

I struggled to follow. It was simply more delicate crampon work and a finer balancing act than I felt capable of. Furthermore, the tension traverse that Mark had used was not available to me, because I had to remove the cam before I could commence the long move back right.

I ventured across, nonetheless. The further I got, the more precarious things felt. One crampon disengaged, I scrambled to secure it again, then the other gave way too and I was off. I fell in a big arc, an alarming sense of free fall, until happily I was caught by a further well-placed cam off to the right. I pulled myself together, telling myself out loud to stay calm. Using my Ropeman (a cambered prusiking device for ascending a rope), I climbed back up almost within reach of the second cam; then the friction went, and I fell back down violently with the Ropeman still in my hand.

Up I went again, and this time reached and removed the cam. But once more I couldn't hold myself and fell a third time in another huge arc, crashing with real force on to my left knee and backside. I was in pain. I fought again to stay calm and conducted a sort of bodily audit of my various faculties to establish the extent of the damage. The truth was that I remained remarkably unscathed. No broken anything, just a lot of bruised, sore parts. I resumed climbing. The fun was not yet over and there were some further committing pitches, but eventually we reached the comparative security of the Second Ice Field.

By this stage a beautiful sunset was unfolding beneath us. In the west we could see the sun for the first time that day as it lowered gently into a sea of cotton-wool clouds, through which pierced just the very tops of the neighbouring rocky peaks. Then the light failed rapidly.

Mark was above me putting in ice screws to protect our ascent. I continued upwards. The Second Ice Field is notorious for icefall and rockfall. Climbing with Chris Bonington at this same point in 1962 during the first British ascent of the Face, Ian Clough described trying to make himself 'as small a target as possible, receding into my crash helmet as a frightened tortoise does into his shell.'[2] He escaped the stonefall; as we have seen, I wasn't quite so lucky. There was an adrenaline rush as ice and rock crashed on to my helmet, shoulders and nearly numb hands. But we survived that incident to reach, and regroup at, the upper edge of the ice field.

It was now well after dark and the priority was to find a bivouac. We improvised where we were. It wasn't spacious, but with a bit of digging out of the ice, there was room for Mark to lie down and me to slouch seated. By this stage, we had been climbing continuously for fifteen and a half hours. We were too tired to cook, so it was melted snow and cereal bars for dinner.

At one point during the night, half our belay failed, and the sacks set off down the mountain. The sacks were attached to us. This was either a good or a bad thing, the determination of which depended very much on whether the remaining belay held. Fortunately it did, and we were able to haul the sacks back in. But from then on, a couple of small nuts were all that kept the two of us and all our equipment in situ. I had never had to cope with an unplanned, improvised bivouac like this. I did cope, but not well. Indeed, I had quite a faff before settling down in my sleeping bag with my inflatable mattress folded under my backside. Wearing all my clothes, including boots and helmet, I was still cold. The previous year I had thought the Swallow's Nest a tight bivouac, but it was five-star compared to this. Still, by pushing on we had put ourselves in a much better position for the morrow. And the weather seemed to be holding.

At 5.30 a.m. Mark turned to me and muttered, 'Oh, are you still here?' Fair comment, considering the quality of our belay and the precarious nature of my position. Packing up needed great care and took us an hour and a half. We brewed tea and folded up mats and bags, while strapping on crampons and other gear. This is a remarkably stressful process, because one false move can send a critical piece of kit down the Face. Lose a single axe and the attempt is all but over; lose the stove or a crampon, and all bets are off.

There was, however, one reassuring feature. A notable characteristic of these lower bivouacs on the North Face is the familiar sounds from below. Noise carries so easily up the Eiger that on much of its Face we could hear the animal bells and raised voices from the valley. It was quite eerie, but comforting, too.

On our way once again, we found a difficult but manageable route across the top of the Second Ice Field. From there we could access the so-called Flatiron, named after its shape. Here we zigzagged up some testing rock and ice pitches. On one we were forced to depend on an old fixed rope, which eventually revealed it had only two puny strands still in place. A lucky escape. There was a steep ice pitch, then it mellowed and much easier ground brought us to a snowy shoulder with overhanging rocks on the right.

This was Death Bivouac. The first attempt on the North Face of the Eiger, by two Munich climbers in 1935, ended here, where they froze to death. But, despite the grimness of its resultant name, this is actually a comfortable shelf, narrow but long, well overhung and therefore protected. It is with little question the best resting place on the upper part of the Face. We spent an hour there, brewing up and replenishing water bottles. To these we added electrolytes which helped balance our fluid intake and retention. We could happily have rested there longer but, as always, time was pressing.

We dropped off the shoulder on to the Third Ice Field. This is steep and exposed ground, but we found reasonable ice for the long traverse left on to the Ramp. This latter feature was a good deal steeper than I had anticipated or than its name might suggest. And it offered some hard rock climbing, up chimneys with dinner-plate ice that shattered uselessly when hit with an axe.

At the top of the Ramp lay the Waterfall Pitch, a cascade of frozen ice clinging to the mountainside, magnificent and daunting. Here it was in 1952 that Hermann Buhl, the leading Austrian climber of his generation, had struggled for so long to overcome the 'ice bulge'. Here too on that same occasion, Gaston Rébuffat had accepted the rope lowered to him rather than risk a second lead. Born in Marseille and brought up climbing on the cliffs of the Calanques on the French Mediterranean coast, Rébuffat had, six years earlier, become the first non-Chamoniard ever to be admitted into Chamonix's Compagnie des Guides. Buhl and Rébuffat's combined teams comprised nine Alpinists: two Austrians, two Germans, four Frenchmen and an Italian. And thus was formed the first truly European team to climb the Face. Although judging by their subsequent, not entirely consistent, accounts of the climb, it was a team perhaps characterised more by mutual respect than deep affection – more *realpolitik* than *entente cordiale.*

It was late in the afternoon when we reached this icy barrier, and Mark's initial thought was to wait and tackle it in the morning. We found a possible bivouac site, but I was concerned about its exposure to stonefall. Mark tried higher up and, in the course of doing so, committed himself to some difficult ground. He didn't fancy reversing it, which was fair enough, and anyway none of these bivouac sites really felt right. Before we knew it, we were pushing on.

The ascent of the Waterfall Pitch seemed to me technically the most difficult part of the climb. Mark led without his pack. Every placement he made with axe or crampon on this frozen chandelier just led to a shower of glass: ice crashing and tinkling down on me below. It seemed like nothing would hold and I felt sure it was only a matter of time before Mark would come hurtling down along with the debris.

There was gear in to protect a fall, but it was of dubious quality. If Mark did fall, he would take a bang. Would he be OK? And even if he was, what on earth would we do then? There appeared to be little water ice left to climb. There was an alternative rock route, but it looked well beyond our abilities – it had certainly confounded the combined efforts of Buhl and his partner, Sepp Jöchler.

Somehow Mark defied gravity. I had never seen him climb like that before. As he later described it, there was 'no opportunity to doubt'. At one point his crampons came completely away and he was hanging free on two ice picks. Only a one-arm pull-up saved him. It was a superhuman effort. And then all of a sudden there was a reverberating cheer and he had done it. Or at least he thought he had. There was still a pretty tough pitch on unconsolidated snow above, but either way he was soon at a belay and bringing me up.

My own climb was not without difficulty: I had a top rope, but also two packs to handle. Crucially I found a jam for my axe, but I too struggled with the unconsolidated snow. Mark and I ended up together at a very wet belay, water pouring from above and night falling equally rapidly. It was, to add to everything, one of the few moments of route-finding doubt that we had on the Face.

We eventually found a short descent to the right that led to a cave, from which I belayed Mark as he climbed steeply up and slightly left. This was without question the worst belay I had ever had to manage. All my weight was suspended on a single ice screw. The sixty-metre ropes were so twisted that I could feed out only a few inches at a time, with the constant fear that any moment they would jam entirely. Radio contact between us was working only intermittently. And it was now dark, with just the dull light of my headlamp to work by. It couldn't have been worse.

But it got worse. Suddenly I felt a searing pain in my left hip. It was unbearable. I didn't think I could move but I simply had to. I cried out, but there was only myself to hear. The pressure of my harness from endless weighted belays had finally taken its toll on my hips. Somehow I shifted my weight, somehow I kept the rope feeding out, somehow Mark continued climbing above. The one thing I knew was that I had to get out of that cave.

Eventually the call came, and I began to climb. I experienced whimpering relief as the pressure came off my harness and once more my legs bore my weight. The route went up steep ice, made trickier because my headlamp was repeatedly knocked out of position by rocks overhead. Then things eased with comforting, reliable *névé* to bury my picks in. We emerged on to the steep snow slope that leads up to the Brittle Ledges. We knew there was a bivouac site close above us, but in the darkness we were unable to find it. It was already midnight. We had no choice but to bivouac where we were, digging out two bucket-seats in the forty- to fifty-degree slope.

There was the usual challenge of securing kit with ice screws and getting into puffball jackets and sleeping bags without dropping anything. The ropes were spread all over the mountain but there was little we could do about that. Suddenly the bivouac of the previous night didn't seem so bad after all. We did eat, though – our first hot meal in two days: couscous and olive oil.

It was an amazing position. I looked down the snow slope to a field of stars. It had been, in Mark's words, a quality mountain day, and our sixteen hours of climbing (7 a.m. to midnight less an hour's rest at Death Bivouac) had put us in pole position for the coming day. Despite all, we were in high spirits and somehow found ourselves at 2.30 a.m. discussing of all things Sartre and existentialism!

... But then Sartre did have a lot to say that was relevant to climbing (sort of), or at least to that timeless question 'Why do we climb?' He answered this implicitly by posing another question: 'Why do anything?' Or as Monty Python would have it, 'What is the meaning of life?' Sartre's answer, expounded at great length in his opaque and difficult-to-read *Being and Nothingness*, turns out to be quite simple: the meaning of your life is whatever meaning you choose to give it. Only you can decide. This is a theme that can be traced back in time through the works of Nietzsche, Dostoyevsky and even the devoutly religious Kierkegaard. Some of a shallower religious disposition might cite 'God's will', but the Christian Kierkegaard recognised that was just a cop-out. No, for Kierkegaard and others, that wouldn't do. An appeal to a higher power is just an abdication of personal responsibility. Nor can one's purpose be solely to help others, for that merely begs the question, what is one helping them to achieve? It only kicks the intellectual can down the road. In short, each individual must shape his or her own purpose in life; that purpose being expressed through the life projects he or she chooses to pursue. If one of those projects happens to be climbing, then that is as valid a choice as any other. And that's about all there is to be said of the validity of climbing as a pursuit ... although Rosemary I'm sure would have further observations to add. I would love to say that, with such comforting thoughts, I drifted off to sleep, but I didn't. Well, maybe I dozed for an hour or so, but it was no more than that. Considering how easily I fell asleep when I was actually reading *Being and Nothingness*, it was a little disappointing!

We were up at 5.30 a.m. and away at 7 a.m. Below us lay a sea of puffy valley clouds with mountaintops protruding like islands in a foaming sea. It was a moment of great beauty. There is a magnificence about the Eigerwand, but it remains a terrible magnificence whatever its aesthetics. Its sheer size alone is daunting. Sepp Jöchler said, 'If one compares the stature of man with that of the Face, man simply disappears.'[3] Indeed.

As we left camp, an incident occurred that illustrated how narrow was the gap between success and failure. The rope linking Mark and me caught on one of my near-buried axes, lifted it, and dropped it down the mountainside. It caught, fortunately, on the hard morning snow, but teetered there, threatening to continue its journey into the valley below. I cried out to Mark to hold still, climbed carefully down and retrieved it. Oh, so close!

In the light of dawn, we saw, of course, where we should have bivouacked, but daytime is daytime and night is night.

The first challenge of the new day was the rock pitch called the Brittle Ledges. This was not a great deal easier than the Difficult Crack, but our teamwork by now was solid and we soon got Mark up there. I followed with the luggage. These ledges are the key to the upper part of the mountain, and I guess for the first time I really dared think we would make it. Mark's emotions were running higher still. The top of the Brittle Ledges is the start of a great traverse and this was as far as Mark had ever climbed in any of his previous ten or so attempts. It was here, twenty years earlier, that he had sat on a ledge for five days waiting for a storm to pass so that he could be rescued by helicopter.

The Traverse of the Gods was without doubt my favourite place on the Eiger. It leads rightwards over an initially wide but steeply sloping snow ledge that becomes ever narrower and more precarious. As Mark commented afterwards, 'It got more godlike the further you went. You could see Grindelwald between the ice on your front points.' There is a vertical kilometre drop from the Traverse to the pastures of Alpiglen below, and it feels like it. Hermann Buhl, half a century ago, thought 'its only association with the Gods seemed to be the idea of making a rather abrupt acquaintance with them.'[4] There is indeed an extraordinary feeling of exposure. The sheer verticality is, at one and the same time, intimidating and exhilarating. Of course, it makes no difference whether you fall a hundred metres or ten times that, but ten times that still feels a very long way! The climbing was good, though. There were solid rock holds and belays and firm ice, with an occasional fixed rope thrown in too.

And then, almost too soon, it was behind us and we were at the iconic upper ice field, known from Heinrich Harrer's book of the same name as the White Spider – so called because the snow here gathers in indents in the rock to form an eerie sprawling pattern like a spider's web. Harrer's book charts a history of the notorious face, known variously as the Eigerwand, Nordwand or, ominously, Mordwand ('murder wall'). Its centrepiece is an account of the first ascent in 1938 by a joint party of Germans and Austrians, a party in which Harrer played a key role. It was that same 1938 route that we had been following, and here we were at last at its focal point.

The Spider, 'that perpetual, fearfully steep field of frozen snow,'[5] made a deep impression on Harrer: 'The "White Spider" on the Eiger is the extreme test not only of a climber's technical ability, but of his character as well. Later on in life, when fate seemed to spin some spider's web or other across my path, my thoughts often went back to the "White Spider".'[6]

I must admit that the Spider was smaller than I had expected and much less fearsome. No debris was coming down it and we even stopped in its middle for a bite to eat and a drink. This was almost the only place on the Eiger where Mark and I consistently moved together. The *névé* was excellent and we felt perfectly secure. But conditions vary greatly, and Harrer was clearly there on a different day.

We exited the Spider at the top right and continued moving together up snow and ice gullies diagonally left, which brought us ultimately to the Quartz Crack. This was initially ice: 'It's Scottish Grade V – I'm in my element!' Mark exclaimed. But then it turned to rock and a narrow rib-buster of a chimney. And, on cue, I did bust my rib – or at least bruised it sufficiently that I wasn't able to raise my voice for the rest of the trip. Mark may have welcomed that!

From the Quartz Crack we traversed left. Once again it was getting late. The Eigerwand spends most of the day brooding in its own shadow, but for the last hour or so before dark the sun skirts around enough to the west to catch its angled slopes with a brilliant evening light. For this brief moment in its daily routine, the Face seems to smile as the rock at last warms a little. On this occasion, it became almost too warm, cosseted as we were in our multiple layers of clothing. Fortunately, the traverse offered some running water and we took a grateful drink. By this stage our food was rarely more than power gels. These proved an important aid. They are essentially liquid calories. You can grab one from a pocket with one hand, rip off the top with your teeth and put them down your throat without ever releasing your grip with the other hand. They won't put the Roux brothers out of business, but they do the job.

A short descent via a tension traverse brought us to the Corti Bivouac, named after Claudio Corti, the young Italian climber who bivouacked there for many days in 1957, the last survivor of a rope of four. Corti was the first man ever rescued from the Face. His rescuer, Alfred Hellepart, descended from the summit ridge by winch and cable and thus earned a unique view of 'this grim, menacing blackness, broken only by a few snow ledges, falling sheer and endlessly away into illimitable depths … space between heaven and hell … that terrible wall.'[7]

One major difficulty now lay ahead of us: the Exit Cracks. These are actually a succession of gullies or open chimneys. The first started as a wide waterfall but became increasingly demanding the further you climbed. Thankfully there was some ice that we could get our axe points into. Without that it would have seemed insurmountable – and Mark was on a seriously long runout before he found that ice. Then the belay rope jammed just as he was making his last-gasp reach for the top. He yelled for rope and, after a worrying hiatus, at last it freed and he found safety. The gullies went on, but none was as tough as that first one. Eventually we emerged in the fading light on to a tiny ridge with the Summit Snow Field to our right.

It was getting dark, but there could be no stopping now. I was very tired and was struggling to manage the rope. Mark felt it most sensible for us to move together, with him placing ice screws for protection, but this became riskier as the ground got steeper and the ice thinner.

We strapped on our head torches and set about a tiring, dark, rather lonely and foreboding climb up that final slope. But we kept going, knowing the best chance of a decent bivouac lay at the top. And yet with every step, I was drawing closer to total exhaustion.

In the darkness, Mark felt the presence of another person, as though he were climbing there with us. Apparently, this is a common phenomenon for those alone in remote places. After all, we had not seen another human being since we had climbed on to the Face; not even a single footprint. As T.S. Eliot described it so poignantly in *The Waste Land*:

Who is the third who walks always beside you?
When I count, there are only you and I together
But when I look ahead up the white road
There is always another one walking beside you[8]

At 10 p.m. I joined Mark on the Mittellegi Ridge. Although not on the summit proper, we had completed the ascent of the North Face. We had climbed that day for fifteen hours.

Mark had already phoned his wife, Jane, and I was keen to reach Rosemary. I gave him my home number to key into his phone. No recognition. We tried a variant. Same problem. It was only on the third attempt that I got my own home phone number right. I was even more tired than I thought. Unfortunately, by this stage the signal had died. I would have to try later. In the meantime, Jane would pass on the news that we had made it and were OK.

It was another 'snow bucket' bivouac, this time on the south side of the mountain. The snow was softer, which made it easier for me to dig large beds for Mark and myself. We couldn't lie down properly, but we could curl up in the foetal position. However, the downside of the softer snow was that there was no chance to secure ice screws. The axes could be depended upon to hold our packs, but not us. We had to rely on not rolling out of our bunks. The steepness of the slope where we were was only forty to fifty degrees, but close below us it dropped off more sharply, and a slide in a sleeping bag would have been near impossible to arrest. The point was drilled home when I accidentally knocked Mark's plastic mug. That was the last we saw of it. I don't know how many hours I slept, but it was not a lot. I couldn't get the thought out of my mind: if I turned over, I'd be dead! Not conducive to slumber.

We made a leisurely start the next morning. There was no doubt we were thinking 'lie in, easy day' … so it was a rude awakening when we set off up the Mittellegi Ridge at a relaxed 8 a.m. I had climbed this ridge once before, during my east–west traverse of the mountain, but it was different now. Apparently, there had been only four climbing days on this route all summer, and we could see why. The ridge was a knife-edge. We tiptoed along it, conscious of terminal drops to either side. The only hope of saving a fall by one climber would be for the other to leap off the other side of the ridge. An unattractive option, but better than the alternative!

At last we reached the 3,970-metre summit of the Eiger. It was 9 a.m. Another special moment. And a view of two worlds. The Eigerwand's reputation for bad weather was easy to comprehend from this high vantage point. To the south loomed the still larger mountains of the Oberland, among them the Mönch, the Jungfrau and, highest of them all, the Finsteraarhorn. But to the north the land fell quite sharply away to the comparatively low-lying valley of Interlaken, with Lucerne beyond. As a result, any weather systems coming from the north struck the north wall of the Eiger first with unmitigated force.

We had made it, but there remained the task of getting down. We elected to descend the South Ridge rather than the easier West Face, because the navigation would be more certain. It also added to the aesthetic appeal, allowing us to complete the traverse.

We had expected it to be well travelled and in good condition, but it was neither. We dropped down the ridge, a mixture of climbing and abseiling. At the col, we rested for an hour. There we melted snow for water, and I tended my feet. Then there was more front-pointing, which I found desperately tiring, and some moderate rock climbing.

Eventually we broke off the ridge and on to the glacier. And there came the final twist of the Eiger knife. There was no track, just knee-deep soft snow. It was agonising. Mark pleaded to the heavens for a firm foothold, but to no avail. Nor were the objective dangers over. The fresh snow was hiding the mantraps of the glacier and we found one, Mark sinking waist-deep into a crevasse. Fortunately, he extracted himself easily.

We were trying to make the last train from the Jungfraujoch, but the soft snow did for us. We found ourselves at the bottom of the last slope to the final col, but it was all too much. Mark had led every foot of the way up and down that mountain, but even guides eventually get tired. He sank to his knees in the snow and rolled on to his back in exhaustion.

I joined him there. We looked at each other and couldn't help but laugh. Here were the newly self-styled Conquerors of the Eigerwand, unable to climb a gentle snow slope to a simple col. We gave up on the train and settled instead for a night at the Mönchjochhütte, reaching it around 6 p.m. after a ten-hour day. It was our shortest day, but it by no means felt that way.

Although described as a hut, the Mönchjochhütte is actually a four-storey modern building, perched on stilts and protruding defiantly from the rocky ridge. A wonderful welcome awaited us there. Two British guides, Robbie and Murray, well understood what we had been through and set to helping us sort our gear and settle down. They were the first people we had seen in four days. There followed an evening of phone calls home and friendly chatter around the hut's dining tables.

I was in my bunk early. Such comfort felt like paradise. We were safe, although inevitably my feet looked pretty grim. We had worn crampons throughout the whole climb and my boots had stayed on even in my sleeping bag. But I was warm under my rugs. It snowed in the night. Thankfully we were not still out there.

I awoke to the agony and the ecstasy: an ecstasy of the mind; an agony of the body. I was much refreshed and had that jubilant morning-after feeling of 'my God, we did it, we really did it!' In my mind I could have done it all over again, but my body felt otherwise. Having held together through everything the Eiger had thrown at it over four days, it now collapsed. Having scaled the Difficult Crack, Hinterstoisser Traverse, three Ice Fields, Ramp, Waterfall Pitch, Brittle Ledges, Traverse of the Gods, Spider, Exit Cracks and those final Summit Snow Fields, not to mention getting back down again, that body was now obliged to climb the hut staircase one step at a time, clutching the rail for support.

The litany of injuries was long: lacerated fingers from rock climbing, a gashed nose from the icefall and rockfall, bruised ribs from the Quartz Crack, a battered butt and bashed-up knee from the falls above the Ice

Hose, an injured hip from harness pressure, a strained shoulder from who-knows-what, and frostbitten toes from cold nights and all that front-pointing. But more than that there was just physical exhaustion, linked to lack of sleep, weight loss and an excess of exercise.

Could I have kept going had there been a fifth day? Of course the answer is yes. But there wasn't a fifth day, and my body knew it. It had done its bit and it wasn't doing any more. I hobbled around, sorting kit, and joined Mark and the others for breakfast. By this stage the whole hut had learnt of our climb. Given that none of the routes up the Eiger was 'open', the fact that we had just traversed it in such conditions, including an ascent of the Face, created quite a stir. We were the heroes of a doubtless passing moment.

I felt far from heroic, though, as I winced, forcing my now-swollen feet back into those boots. It was such a tight fit that I couldn't tie the laces properly and had to miss out alternate 'eyes'. The short snow plod down to the Jungfraujoch did its best to be enchanting in the rapidly clearing early morning, but I had difficulty appreciating it. I was in pain.

We returned down the mountain as paying customers of the railway rather than potential convicts cowering in the darkness of the tunnel. I must admit I prefer the conventional mode of travel. Before long we were in the rich green pastures of the Grindelwald Valley. After days in the mountains where the eyes grow accustomed to nothing but black and white, that first blast of green always strikes me as wonderful – stepping back into a world of colour.

The Eigerwand certainly didn't mark the end of my passion for the Alps. Many other memorable climbs followed: the Frontier Ridge on Mont Maudit, the North Face of the Aiguille Blanche and the Nant Blanc Face on the Aiguille Verte, all in the Mont Blanc Massif; the Barre des Écrins and Traverse of the Meije in the Dauphiné; the South Face of the Marmolada and the Comici Route on the Cima Grande in the Dolomites;

and the Pallavicini Couloir on the Grossglockner in the Austrian Tyrol to name just a few. And I was active too in my own country, with rock climbs all over the United Kingdom, including, at its northernmost extremity, the Old Man of Hoy – climbed on a rope of three with Mark and Peter Folkman, the friend who had first introduced the two of us.

But the Eigerwand did get me thinking about mountains still further afield. Could there be other routes in more distant places with that same iconic status, that same combination of history, aesthetics and drama?

These thoughts took a little time to incubate and were interrupted by some other risk-taking that went badly wrong – risk-taking that had nothing to do with climbing. Even before our Eiger ascent, things had started to go awry in the world's financial markets. The situation reached its apex a year later with the collapse of the Wall Street investment bank, Lehman Brothers, and the rescue of the Royal Bank of Scotland (RBS). Pessimism was rife. I remember the Chief Economist of RBS being asked if there was any *good* news. The dour Scot looked surprised by the question and responded, 'Jesus loves you.'

At this time, I was serving on the senior leadership team of an investment firm that I had helped establish twenty-three years previously. We now had a team of roughly 200 people in ten offices on three continents, managing what was, for a period at least, the largest private equity fund in the world. But all was not well. Private equity is one of the riskiest investment asset classes. We owned majority, controlling stakes in businesses like Hugo Boss and Valentino that were experiencing collapsing sales. The fund's value was down to thirty-eight per cent of cost. This in turn placed huge pressure on our own investors, the largest of which in October 2008 threatened to default and force the fund into liquidation. In effect, this would spell the end of the firm that I and others had spent two decades creating. We had placed all our proverbial eggs in one basket. Our mantra had been 'One Firm, One Fund, One Focus'. This now became, in the words of one of my female partners, 'One Fund, One

F**k-up, One Finish'. We would have to negotiate a restructuring of the fund or fold.

As I led the negotiations with our investors and other stakeholders, I often thought back to the situation we had faced on the Second Ice Field of the Eigerwand. Staying calm was critical and, despite my financial and emotional ties to the firm, I needed to maintain a certain objective detachment. Throughout meeting after meeting, I told myself, 'Take it one step at a time. And remember, this is only about business. However badly this turns out, no one is going to die.' We were able to reach agreement; the fund eventually returned the investors' money almost twice over; the firm did survive; and today it is one of the strongest in its industry. That is thanks to many hands other than mine. But I do feel that climb on the Eiger played its part.

By 2012, things had finally settled down. We had raised a new fund and I was confident the future of the firm was secure. Now fifty-three years old, I felt it time to visit the nexus of Asian climbing, some would say of world climbing: Nepal.

Ama Dablam, with the South-West Ridge on the right skyline.

2

ASIA

SOUTH-WEST RIDGE
OF AMA DABLAM
(NEPAL)

Juniper smoke rose from the small altar, curling through rough rocks above, up past fluttering prayer flags into a crisp blue early-morning sky. To the left, waiting to be blessed, lay a pile of climbing equipment including a Black Diamond Couloir Harness of mine. There were gifts of biscuits, rice, soda, a can of Tuborg and a bottle of Johnnie Walker Black Label. In front of them sat cross-legged a lama who had ascended that morning from Tengboche Monastery or Dawa Choling Gompa, an important Tibetan Buddhist monastery of the Sherpa community. Beside the lama sat Dorje Sherpa, the expedition's sirdar or leader, a veteran of fifteen Everest ascents, and next to him our three Western guides. Beyond were gathered the other Sherpas, kitchen staff and expedition members, including me.

The lama worked through his lengthy incantations, reading from a scroll laid between his knees, while the rest of us ritually cast rice into the air. In the background I heard the softly and endlessly repeated chant 'Om mani padme hum'. Apparently it means 'praise to the jewel in the lotus'. You could legitimately ask, 'What does that mean?', but this didn't seem to be the moment. This was no casual ceremony. This was the

Buddhist *puja* to show reverence and ask for blessing on our coming ascent. It was a serious religious ritual for many of our Sherpas – although for others, I noticed, a chance to throw rice down the necks of friends who were sitting in front.

Around *my* neck, a Sherpa tied a thin red thread. It would stay there until I left Nepal. Another Sherpa smeared white powder on my face. Do that in New York and you'd probably be arrested, but here it seemed quite natural. A third Sherpa offered me a sip of *chang*. At 8 a.m. that was quite spirited, I thought, in more ways than one.

Before us towered the object of our supplication: Ama Dablam, described by many as the most beautiful mountain in the world, and not without reason. The name means 'mother's necklace', the overhanging glacier below its summit evoking a traditional Nepalese pendant. This particular necklace seems to threaten to break off at any moment and descend on those unfortunates below, but the dominant feature is more benign. The mountain's two extending ridges, like a mother's arms, seem to embrace all who venture near.

At 6,856 metres, Ama Dablam is not particularly high by Himalayan standards, but it is by far the most technically challenging of the range's popularly climbed peaks. If Everest is the Mont Blanc of the Himalaya, then Ama Dablam is the Matterhorn. It has a particular historic importance, because its first ascent in 1961 marked the beginning of technical alpinism in the Himalaya. George Lowe's prophecy, during the 1953 Everest Expedition, that 'that peak [Ama Dablam] will never be climbed', was of course eventually proven wrong, but not until eight years after the ascent of Everest.[9] Even today, the popular climbers' website Summit Post observes that 'It's common to encounter high altitude Everest veterans having problems with the technical difficulties encountered on the crux pitches of this climb.'[10]

The mountain repulsed early attempts by successive British expeditions in 1958 and 1959, the latter at a cost of two lives. It succumbed eventually to a rather unusual team of mountaineers, a group of scientists/climbers who wintered at the foot of the mountain in a silver Nissan-hut-like construction seven metres long and three metres wide. This 'Silver Hut' was positioned at an altitude of 5,800 metres, thus facilitating near-perfect acclimatisation. The expedition was nominally led by Sir Edmund Hillary, although at the time Hillary was heavily preoccupied by his search for the Himalayan yeti. As a result, leadership of the mountain-eering endeavour fell to Englishman Mike Ward (the expedition doctor from the successful Everest ascent), supported by two New Zealanders and an American. Notwithstanding their exceptional acclimatisation, it still took them three weeks to climb the South-West Ridge, our intended route. Their achievement was considerable, but not well received in all quarters. They had omitted to apply for a permit from the Nepalese authorities to climb the mountain, and Hillary needed all his diplomatic skills to untangle the resulting mess.

After the climb, Mike Ward described Ama Dablam as 'a mountain of Alpine calibre; the route … providing climbing of every variety.'[11] Indeed, the South-West Ridge offers three successive phases: the first steep rock, the second steep ice and the third, well, just steep. One of the other first ascensionists, Barry Bishop, described the mountain's 'cold but beautiful aloofness … a formidable, even frightening challenge'.[12] Definitely a climber's climb. And a natural choice for someone looking for a contest beyond height alone.

We had set out eight days earlier from Kathmandu. We had flown to the mountain village of Lukla, with its alarming downward-sloping runway, and hiked from there to Namche Bazaar, the gateway to the Khumbu Valley which itself unlocks the route to Everest and its neighbouring peaks. This had been my introduction to the world of precipitous wooded gorges, swaying suspension bridges and streaming prayer flags; of chorten and stupa that must be passed only in a clockwise direction, prayer wheels that can be turned only in a clockwise direction, and monasteries that must be circumnavigated only in a clockwise direction. And tea lodges – lots of tea lodges – which could be approached from any direction you chose.

It had been a week without cars, a week that would become a month. In upper Nepal everything inanimate travels on someone else's back, whether that be yak, dzopio (a cross between a cow and a yak) or porter. Since the suspension bridges are exactly one yak wide, this adds extra interest when you meet a yak halfway across.

And then there was Namche Bazaar. Namche is surely the most international and yet most local place on earth: fancy branded mountaineering shops and internet cafés sit alongside Buddhist shrines and villagers washing their clothes in the stream that runs down the main street. You're as likely to hear Swedish spoken as Nepalese. The main bar is run by an imposing lady, Sushi-La, who describes herself as from Kathmandu and New York. I had instantly fallen in love with this unique, crazy place.

Beyond Namche lie the quiet villages of Kunde, Phortse and Khumjung, where we had stayed in tea lodges run by the families of our Sherpas, and visited the hospital and school built by Hillary and the Himalayan Trust. At the school, in return for a modest donation, I had been given a picture of Ama Dablam painted by one of the younger children. It remains on my wall to this day. Still deeper into the Khumbu Valley, we had spent two nights in the comparatively barren hamlet of Dingboche, and from there climbed the trekking peak Chukkhung-Ri (5,550 metres), with its rocky, flag-strewn summit and its magnificent view of the Lhotse Face and, beyond it, the summit of Everest. Finally, we had crossed a river and returned down the other side of the valley where we had veered off south to the pretty meadow, split by a mountain stream, that serves as Ama Dablam's Base Camp (4,600 metres).

This all felt a very new world, although I had been to the Himalaya once before, three decades previously. With my brother Simon and Rosemary my wife-to-be, I had trekked extensively in the provinces of Kashmir and

Ladakh. As we had crossed the Gongmaru La (5,200 metres), the high point of our final trek, I had knelt one knee in the snow and asked Rosemary to marry me. She had accepted, although she claims to this day that she did so only as the result of oxygen deprivation to the brain. Much has happened in the intervening period, not least the arrival of our three children, Timothy, Tabitha and Tatiana – collectively known as 'the 3 Ts' and carefully named with the same initial, so that their school clothing could be handed down without relabelling. Rosemary is nothing if not practical.

Back in the present, it was now time to move higher and see how the red blood cells would cope on the mountain itself. At 10.15 a.m. I set off slowly up a rather steep hill, then climbed a long ridge with fine views on either side, especially to the left, where Ama Dablam was framed by the ubiquitous prayer flags. At the next ridge, a fierce wind forced me into additional layers of clothing, creating a more authentic Himalayan feel. But this was still very much trekking, and my walking poles were all that was needed to deliver me in two hours and forty-five minutes to Yak Camp.

Yak Camp sits at 5,400 metres and is so called because it's the highest point to which the yaks can carry supplies. Tents dot a stony landscape on terraces that have been scraped out by the Sherpas over the years. The ground is a little bleak, yet surrounded by much grandeur, with snow-capped peaks on all sides.

Most of our team were already established there, and I felt well catered for health-wise, given that the company included a doctor (Jon), a pharmacist (René) and a vet (Stacey). With the addition of an IT consultant (Viki) and a plumber (Stuart), we were prepared for every eventuality.

This was very much an acclimatisation sortie. We spent less than an hour at Yak Camp eating our lunch before descending back to Base Camp for the night – the first in a pattern of outings following the principle of 'climb high, sleep low'.

Before crawling into my tent and sleeping bag back at Base Camp, I took 125 milligrams of Diamox to help smooth my periodic breathing. Periodic breathing, also known as Cheyne–Stokes respiration, is associated with altitude, but is not itself a symptom of altitude sickness. At or near sea level, the trigger for the human body to take a breath is the build-up of excess carbon dioxide. The reduced pressure at high altitude means there is inadequate carbon dioxide to generate this response. Instead the body relies on a backup system triggered by the deficiency of oxygen. However, this creates a delay: the body stops breathing for a period and then gasps as it makes up for the lost breaths. This is not a serious problem health-wise, but it does tend to inhibit sleep. Fortunately, the Diamox did the trick and I slept for nine and a half hours, waking tremendously refreshed.

The morning was splendidly relaxed. Modern Himalayan climbing is rather luxurious: I shaved, showered with a special pump-action shower unit, photographed our yaks (as one does) and answered my emails over the satellite-linked solar-powered group Wi-Fi.

After lunch, Adrian Ballinger, an Englishman now living in California and the owner of Alpenglow, the expedition organiser, took personal charge of our instruction in the art of Himalayan climbing. The popular peaks here are climbed with fixed ropes, thus requiring some different skills from those commonly used in the Alps – specifically: in ascent, jumaring; and in descent, arm-wrapping. Both techniques employ friction on the fixed rope. The jumar is a one-way friction device that locks on to the rope and can be moved upwards but not downwards, thus providing both a safety anchor and, if necessary, an aid in ascent. The arm-wrap is a technique of twisting the rope around the body, again creating friction, this time to control the rate of descent. Add to that the use of a double leash with two karabiners, one of which is always on the fixed rope, together with the familiar art of abseiling, and you've pretty much got it. But you do need to get it, and these skills are best acquired down at camp rather than up on the mountain.

Dinner that evening was enlivened by a guest, a Kiwi, Lydia Bradey. In 1988 Lydia became the first woman to climb Everest without supplemental oxygen. About half our team were male Everesters, but none had done it without extra oxygen. We were duly impressed.

The following day was the first of a crucial five-day rotation through the higher camps designed to familiarise us with the terrain, acclimatise us, and ensure that the right gear was in the right place on the mountain. Jon and I were teamed up and set off a little before midday. Shaking off a cold and so not 100% fit, I was climbing slowly. Nonetheless, we were

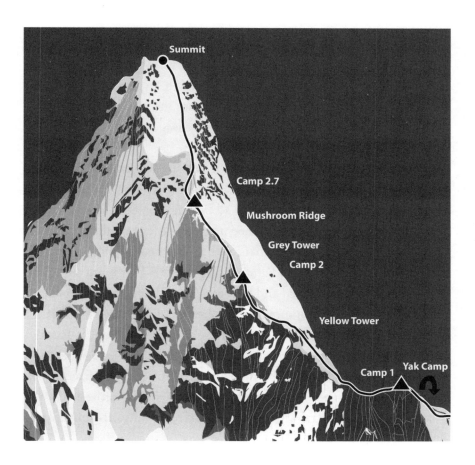

a little faster to Yak Camp than we had been two days earlier. Once there, Jon and I selected one of the team's North Face tents, sorted out the communal equipment that had come up on the yaks – bed mats, sleeping bags and cooking gear – and settled into the business of boiling water. The water had also been brought up by yak, because at this altitude there is no snow. Jon, who had considerably more high-altitude camping experience than I had, took first turn at the cooking.

Then it began to snow. Adrian joked that he would lay on skiing in the morning. Very funny, I thought, as I climbed into my rather modest, zero-degree sleeping bag with most of my clothes on. It was quite a long night.

Jon and I awoke three hours before the group's planned departure and still we weren't ready on time. Melting water for muesli, then more for coffee and yet more for our bottles – added to the usual morning ablutions, getting dressed, putting on harnesses and sorting out backpacks – all proved too much for us. It was a lesson learnt: start early, get organised, keep focused.

Another of the guides, Brian Warren, led us off. A ski and rock-climbing guide from Jackson, Wyoming, he, unlike the other two guides, had come to Ama Dablam with no more acclimatisation than his clients. Yet it certainly didn't show as he stormed up over the icy boulders above Yak Camp. René, a super-fit Dutchman, with a disconcerting likeness to the mad professor in *Back to the Future*, hung in behind with me alongside. But eventually we both tired and fell back. The others were more distant still. We regrouped two hours later, where the hiking trail ended at the foot of some impressive cliffs. There for the first time I put on my harness. Away went the walking poles and out came the jumar and double leash with karabiners. This would be my true initiation into the fixed ropes, hauling myself up these relatively featureless slabs. In fairness it was a reasonably gentle start: sharp, but short. Given the thin air, though, I was well exercised by the top.

Now for the first time we joined the South-West Ridge proper, where an apparently endless stream of colourful prayer flags fluttered high in the brisk wind. With them came a dramatic view down the ridge, which was narrow and rocky at first, but broadened out into a gentle shoulder lower down before halting abruptly at the foot of the neighbouring peaks. On either side the valleys fell away, creating a near unbroken panorama through 270 degrees. Only the summit of Ama Dablam itself interrupted the view.

This, at 5,800 metres, was Camp 1: a series of largely orange tents (climbers are somewhat chromatically limited in their ambition) perched on the easterly flank of the ridge. It was now midday. We deposited as much gear as we could manage without, enjoyed an hour of respite, and then returned the way we had come for a second night at Yak Camp.

This time I took charge of the stove, boiling water for lunch, dinner, drinks and bottles, plus some to be left in the pans for the morning. I cannot claim to be a cook. Indeed, Rosemary despairingly classifies her husband as a 'domesticity-free zone' – part of that public-boarding-school generation, born in a past age, that transitioned seamlessly from doting mother to school matron to college bedder and then to wife and secretary without ever fully appreciating the essential role these people play. It's certainly true that, put in a large, well-equipped kitchen, I have a tendency to panic – the larger and better equipped, the greater the anxiety. But squeezed under the flysheet of a small tent, I rather come into my own, making a somewhat better fist of things. So, in short, we fared pretty well.

Meanwhile, the wind that had buffeted the canvas around us happily subsided overnight. The next morning was like Groundhog Day – a repeat of the previous twenty-four hours, but sleeping at higher altitude at the end. I lit the stove at 6 a.m. and this time was ready to leave fifteen minutes early.

At Camp 1 there was lying snow, and during the afternoon more arrived, this time directly from the heavens. Jon and I settled into our tent.

45

This higher tent was neither level nor flat. Indeed, there was a significant part of the Himalaya poking through the groundsheet. I didn't sleep well, but it wasn't a disastrous night. Jon, on the other hand, described it as the worst night he'd ever had – this from a man who had slept on the South Col of Everest!

Things didn't improve with the morning. We awoke to the news that Brian, our guide, was sick and needed to descend. The head guide, Adrian, was already higher on the mountain with another client. The third guide was down in Base Camp, recuperating from a previous climb. The fact was that we were going nowhere: an enforced rest day at Camp 1.

With Brian gone, a tent was freed up, so Jon and I made the most of it and enjoyed the relative luxury of a tent each. This enabled us to avoid the worst of the 'Himalaya-hump' that night, and find relatively level ground to sleep on.

The weather had changed, though. It was now snowing heavily. I made sure everything that could freeze was in my sleeping bag with me: my contact lenses, sun lotion, toothpaste, socks, inner boots, camera, phone and of course water bottles – filled with boiling water to warm my toes. Given that I had most of my clothes on, there actually wasn't much that *wasn't* in my sleeping bag but, despite all these inanimate bedfellows, I slept well.

I was ready to go at 6 a.m. Clearly I was getting the hang of this early-morning start thing. Adrian was now with us, but given that we numbered six clients, he understandably wanted our third guide in support. That guide was Chad Peele, a first-class ice climber from Colorado. He reached us from Base Camp shortly after 7 a.m. and we set off together up the South-West Ridge on to new ground.

Normally this would have been dry rock, but in the current conditions it was covered with a treacherous coat of snow and ice. As Adrian expressed it over the radio to Base Camp, 'It feels like f**king Christmas up here.' Almost immediately I slid off the slab, and only the fixed rope and my jumar saved me from a one-way trip down the mountain. Another of those lessons.

Adrian led the way, with me behind, then René. René and I were already establishing ourselves as something of a 'front pair'. The others followed, with Chad bringing up the rear. This was not a race, but it made sense for everybody to progress at their own preferred pace. The route traversed the slope, then climbed steeply up to rejoin the ridge. This involved two sections of full-on jumaring. For a climber used to the Alps, the temptation was to rely on the upwards-only, one-way friction of the jumar as just a backup, and attempt to climb properly with hands and feet. This proved highly inefficient. Adrian was soon yelling from above, 'Charles, stop trying to rock-climb!' In response I grabbed the jumar and relied solely on that, hauling myself up the rope. This proved equally inefficient – and even more exhausting. It took me a while to figure it out, but the correct technique was to rely on the feet as much as possible, exploiting every hold available, and to employ the arms predominantly on the jumar, using it for balance and security and, only when necessary, for upward momentum. I got there in the end.

Once back on the ridge, the route became even more mixed, with alternating sections of rock and snow. As with all classic ridges, the view was spectacular on both sides, but today it was made all the more so by the thin layer of fresh snow, sparkling in the sunshine. Airy and somewhat magical. The conditions made it quite testing, though, and we were all tired by mid-morning when the route finally veered a second time from the ridge. It teetered along an invigorating hand traverse right, to the foot of the infamous Yellow Tower.

The Yellow Tower, although short, is the toughest section of rock on the ridge and, in the opinion of many, the crux of the technical climbing. On a dry, sunny day at sea level it would present a comparatively easy challenge for an experienced rock climber, but that's a 'T-shirt, rock shoes and chalk bag' assessment. We had double boots, gloves and big packs, and were climbing at near 6,000 metres. The pitch's twenty-five vertical metres were not made any easier on this particular morning by the addition of a fine layer of verglas, neatly filling in all the cracks.

Adrian attacked it first – and made it look none too straightforward. René arrived just before I set off in pursuit. He had climbed all but one of the sixty-four Alpine 4,000ers and was a veteran of the Seven Summits. He looked at the route ahead, turned to me and said, 'I don't know if I can do this.'

Encouragingly, I passed on Adrian's parting words: 'Climb as quickly as you can, don't rest, keep going till you puke.' That cheered René no end. With that, up I went. Finding any purchase on the verglassed rock was challenging, as was gripping it with gloved hands. I was soon breathing hard as I fought to maintain my stance, let alone make upward progress. All the time the weight of my pack was pulling me backwards off the vertical rock. But there was always the option to rest on the jumar and I took it gratefully. Slowly, very slowly, I did make headway. René followed and of course he managed it too, although neither of us was exactly as fresh as a daisy at the top. Two gasping, wheezing old men would be a fairer description.

Adrian remained to belay the others up the Yellow Tower while René and I climbed on, and shortly reached Camp 2 (6,050 metres). This must be one of the most photographed high camps in the Himalaya. It's spectacularly situated on a craggy knoll protruding from the main ridge, with tents perched on the very top at preposterous angles, their occupants apparently defying gravity. For a few minutes, I had this strange rock bastion to myself, and it felt like a special privilege. Soon René was with me and we deposited our ice-climbing gear in the expedition's one tent. Sadly, Camp 2 is so confined that it has become unsanitary over the years, and attempts to clean it up have proved unsuccessful so far. As a result, we wouldn't be staying there. But we did have the one tent in which to cache equipment, including an extra stove and two sleeping bags in case of emergency.

This was as far as we would climb for now. We left at 11.15 a.m. and down-climbed to the top of the Yellow Tower. Others of the team were still coming up this test-piece and were clearly getting their full entertainment value from the experience. Viki brought up the rear. She looked tired, but was still smiling.

We abseiled the Tower and regrouped at its base. From there Chad led four of us down the ridge with a mix of arm-wraps, down-climbing and further abseils. Descent on this kind of terrain was highly familiar to René and me, who had climbed extensively in the Alps, but less so to the others, who were more versed in big snowy mountains. Furthermore, at 1.30 p.m. it again started to snow. As a consequence, our group moved slowly – but not nearly as slowly, it turned out, as the remaining party further behind.

At Camp 1, we cached further gear, then continued down, regrouping briefly at Yak Camp before descending again to Base Camp. Only René and I reached the latter in the light. Jon, Stacey and Stuart were not that far behind, but it was a further two hours before Viki rolled in, very tired … yet still smiling. It had been a tremendous five days. We had been up over 6,000 metres, had thoroughly familiarised ourselves with the lower half of the mountain, had stashed the equipment at the relevant camps, and had substantially improved our acclimatisation.

But at a cost. Next day the team gathered around the dining table at Base Camp for a debrief. Viki had an announcement: she had decided not to attempt the summit. The descent the previous day had tested her to the full and she felt it would be unwise to venture higher on the mountain. A disappointing, but clearly mature, decision.

The rest of the day was spent sorting kit, shaving and showering, and responding to emails. Rosemary and I had a long chat over the phone. This had proved difficult in recent days – not because of the mobile reception in the Khumbu, but because of the mobile reception where Rosemary was, in darkest Hay-on-Wye in Wales. The ironies of modern communications!

A second rest day followed. We settled on the final teams. Jon and Adrian would climb separately; the remaining four clients (including me) would be with Chad and Brian. Now it was just a question of weather, puff and a bit of luck. On the weather front, at least, the forecast was strong.

The first day of our three-day summit bid started like any other at Base Camp, with the rather fine tradition of 'Sherpa tea', the kitchen team circulating the tents with hot towels and sweet, milky tea. A real treat, much appreciated by all. The sun hit the tents at 7.40 and the happy campers emerged to be welcomed by the head cook, Tashi, and a breakfast of porridge, fruit, omelette, toast and fresh-ground coffee. Tashi was very much a core member of the team. His wife and three children lived in Pokhara, Nepal's second-largest city, but he spent much of the year either high in the Himalaya or as a chef in Gstaad in the Swiss Alps. He could conjure anything from spaghetti bolognese to grilled pork chops, baked salmon and roast lamb. As you will surmise, this wasn't exactly the austerity end of camping. It may sound indulgent, but I learnt that eating well and staying healthy was half the battle in these remote, high mountains.

We headed up the hill after breakfast. Again, the team worked on the sensible theory that everybody moves at their own pace and so, rather than ascend in an enforced huddle, we all set off at our preferred time and at whatever speed suited us. For me that was slowly, at 10 a.m., and with many halts to photograph Ama Dablam. The mountain was looking particularly majestic in the low-angled light of morning. Were the mountain's two encircling arms reaching out to embrace me or to swallow me? I wasn't quite sure. Slow as I was, I eventually caught up with René, and together we arrived at Yak Camp at 12.45 p.m. There we collected our helmets and harnesses. After a short break for a picnic lunch, we continued up and reached Camp 1 in good time to prepare food and water for the afternoon and evening ahead. I turned my headlamp off at 7 p.m., but for some reason slept poorly – perhaps it was nerves.

With the snow now cleared off the ridge, the climbing above Camp 1 next morning went much more smoothly. I'm sure the improved acclimatisation helped too. Chad pushed the pace a bit, which suited most of us, but I noticed Stacey starting to lag. Although an experienced climber, her native Cascade mountains had tested her only at limited altitudes. She was clearly struggling in the thinning air.

We reached the foot of the Yellow Tower at 9 a.m. and this time I climbed it with some gusto, enjoying the challenge of ascending swiftly, but searching out the footholds to minimise the amount of hauling on the jumar. But I arrived at the top to find my elation deflated by disappointing news. Over the radio we heard that Stacey had decided, in her own words, 'to bail'. The altitude and the terrain had taken their toll and she felt muscularly exhausted. Not entirely surprising, since Ama Dablam is a physical climb – but a great shame, because she had been so steady up until then. Guides aside, our party was now three.

Chad, René and I soon reached our previous high point at Camp 2 and retrieved our cached gear. I put my mask and down mitts in my pack, strapped my axe on its outside, and stepped into my overboots and crampons. We rested for an hour, allowing Brian and Stuart to catch up, then set off.

The next section was the so-called Grey Tower: a mix of grey rock and glistening ice. None of it was quite as hard as the Yellow Tower, but it took much longer and demanded far more stamina. The required technique was similar: careful positioning of the feet, albeit now with crampons, and judicious use of the jumar. Judicious or not, it proved sapping. The route was often vertical to near-overhanging, and at that altitude I was soon breathing deeply.

We continued up steeply, occasionally traversing left, until we emerged on to the comparatively level Mushroom Ridge, a gently rising series of enormous snowy pillows that covered the mid-section of the South-West Ridge. In icy conditions this might have presented a real obstacle, with the threat of serious drops on either side. But with relatively warm weather, I was able to stroll along comfortably, marvelling at this spectacular mass of snow balanced on the narrower rock of the ridge beneath, rather like an oversized scoop of ice-cream poised atop a cornet.

The route now trended up and right. As we peered ahead, we glimpsed a flash of orange. It was the tents at Camp 2.7 (6,300 metres). Following the first ascent of this ridge in 1961, expeditions traditionally placed their high camp (Camp 3) on the shoulder of the South-West Ridge, just below the vast overhanging glacier of the Dablam. That was until November 2006, when a huge chunk of the Dablam broke off and wiped out the tents below, killing six climbers. Since then, most expeditions have preferred either to climb from Camp 2 or to pitch their tents just off the ridge, dug into the snow slope to create a protective overhang. This was our Camp 2.7.

There were a couple of things that immediately struck me on arrival. First, the camp was not spacious. The excavated ledge of snow, carved like a cave into the cliff, provided room for three tents only. Second, the terrain was steep, and any sortie outside, day or night, without a harness and leash to the safety line, was likely to be a one-way affair. This was not the sort of campsite where you plonked your deckchair by the tent door. Arrangements were necessarily cosy. René, Stuart and I had one tent, Brian and Chad a second, and our Sherpas the third.

Clearly an early night was in order. But how to sleep? The ground sloped slightly outwards, so we elected to lie down crossways, heads into the slope and feet towards the edge. This meant, though, that I was the only one with access to the door. Not an insuperable problem, because there was no question of any of us actually venturing out from the tent. But it did mean that I took on the dual roles for the group of both chef and pee-bottle emptier, handling both inward consumption and outward production – a sort of general remit for liquid management. One gets to know one's companions rather well in this kind of environment. Stuart, the plumber, had made an elementary error, particularly surprising given his profession. He had brought with him a pee bottle of inadequate capacity. Remedying this necessitated very fine teamwork. Stuart would start the natural process of filling the bottle, but then have to hit the pause button as the bottle's capacity was reached. He'd then pass it (carefully!) to me so I could empty it out of the tent door and return it swiftly into place to receive the rest. On such partnerships are lasting friendships formed. But it was not a great night. With three of us squeezed into the one tent at that altitude, it was never likely to be so. I cannot recall anything one would describe as sleep.

Come the morning, I was taking no chances and fired up the stove at the seemingly early hour of 2.50 a.m. It didn't really matter what time it was; we were all awake anyway. Breakfast was muesli and hot chocolate. Dressing didn't take long because we were wearing most of our clothes already, but packing up was a bit of a performance. Getting into harness, double boots, overboots and crampons all presented their individual difficulties when standing up was not possible.

At 5 a.m. we leaned out of the tent to clip our karabiners into the safety line, and then struggled through the opening into the darkness, the only light at this stage generated by our headlamps. In addition to our two Western guides, each of us would have a Sherpa to assist us in the final ascent above Camp 2.7. René would climb with Nima Sherpa, Stuart with our sirdar (lead Sherpa) Dorje, and I with Kharma Sherpa. Kharma was twenty-four, came from the village of Phortse (where we had stayed the night), spoke almost no English and had summited Everest four times. The Sherpas had been working immensely hard throughout the trip, fixing new ropes and stocking the high camps, but now they would really come into their own, keeping a watchful eye over their comparatively inexperienced and much less acclimatised clients.

We traversed right from the tents before ascending directly on steep ice and frozen snow. Wearing five layers on my lower body and six on my upper, I was soon overheating … but not for long. The moment we hit the ridge above, all that changed. The wind struck my left side and seemed to suck the heat out of me. First, the little finger in my right hand, the one holding the metal jumar, lost sensation. Then more fingers and the toes on my right foot. I kept my various digits constantly on the move to maintain the blood flow as best I could.

Once on the ridge, we climbed slope after slope, never vertical, but steep enough to make it interesting. Nima and René were out front, maintaining a strong pace. I was in the next group, some twenty metres back, well catered for with Chad immediately ahead of me and Kharma behind. Stuart was with Brian and Dorje quite a long way off, lost in the early grey of dawn.

Soon I was facing another challenge: I was getting tired. My altimeter was showing 6,700 metres, only 150 metres or so below the summit, yet there seemed a lot of mountain still above us. And it was apparent that the air up there didn't include as much oxygen as my body would have felt ideal. I was breathing with indecent enthusiasm. In short, I was running out of puff.

Fortunately, the end was for once nearer than it looked, and some time about 7.30 a.m. we topped out. There was a fairyland feel to the summit (6,856 metres). Barely a rock in sight. Instead all around lay a carpet of soft snow, billowing up here and there in puffy drifts – its gentler parts like bleached sand dunes, its spikier parts like the topping on a lemon meringue pie. There was plenty of room to stomp around. A generous summit by any standards.

Mike Ward and his fellow first ascensionists were greeted with 'a close-up view of the inside of an angry cloud'.[13] In contrast, we had a clear sky and it was now full daylight. Every direction offered a panorama of mountain, hill and valley, but inevitably our eyes were drawn to the

EUROPE

Right Conclusion of our first proper attempt on the North Face of the Eiger, as the author exits the mountain. *Photo: Mark Seaton*

Below Contemplating the Eiger's Waterfall Pitch, probably the crux section of the route.

Mark Seaton on the Traverse of the Gods on the North Face of the Eiger, a vertical kilometre above the pastures of Alpiglen.

Inset The author at the White Spider.
Photo: Mark Seaton

Mark Seaton on the knife-edge of the Mittellegi Ridge on the Eiger. The author is watching from behind, ready to jump the other way should he fall.

Mark Seaton at the summit, the morning of our fourth day on the Eiger.

ASIA

Top left Apprentice monks in Kathmandu.

Above A world without motor vehicles. Everything goes up on someone or some animal's back.

Right The river crossings are not for the faint-hearted.

Below Namche Bazaar, the most local and most international place on Earth.

Ama Dablam: sunset at Base Camp.

Ama Dablam: Camp 1 with the ubiquitous prayer flags.

Right René Bergsma on Ama Dablam's Yellow Tower, the hardest rock climbing on the route. At 6,000 metres with gloves, double boots and big packs, we could have done without the addition of verglas.

Below The author on the steep ice of the Grey Tower, Ama Dablam. Camp 2 is just visible on the ridge below. *Photo: Chad Peele*

Bottom Camp 2, where we stashed emergency gear.

Opposite top Camp 2.7, dug in for protection from potential collapse of the séracs above. These killed six climbers in 2006.

Opposite below Kharma Sherpa and the author on the summit of Ama Dablam with Everest and Lhotse in the background. *Photo: Chad Peele*

NORTH AMERICA

Above A room with a view. Max Biagosch and the author settle down for the night in the Grey Band on El Capitan. *Photo: Andy Kirkpatrick*

Opposite Andy Kirkpatrick on the King Swing. He made it on the fifth pendulum. *Photo: Tom Evans*

Left The author emerging from under the Great Roof.
Photo: Andy Kirkpatrick

Above The author at a belay on the upper part of the *Nose*.
Photo: Max Biagosch

Below Max Biagosch, the author and Andy Kirkpatrick
at the top of El Cap. An amazing feeling of peace.

Top Half Dome seen from the summit of El Cap.

Above Andy Kirkpatrick and the author on the descent. We weren't travelling light.
Photo: Max Biagosch

Right The author, Andy Kirkpatrick and Max Biagosch posing in front of the *Nose*, with a nod to an historic valley photograph involving some of the legends of old.
Photo: unknown

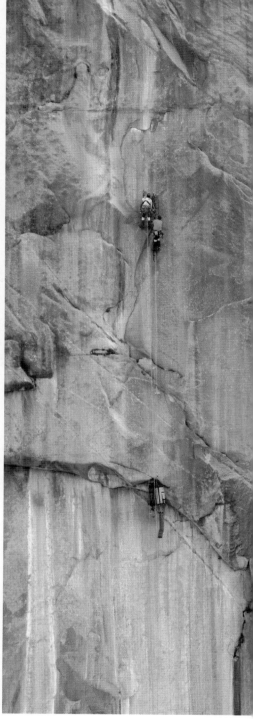

Top left Leaning Tower, Yosemite: supposedly America's steepest rock face (it leans the wrong way).

Above The author and Andy Kirkpatrick on the mid-section of *Zodiac*. *Photo: Tom Evans*

Left Andy Kirkpatrick in descent from Leaning Tower.

The author leading on the upper section of
Moonlight Buttress, Zion. *Photo: Andy Kirkpatrick*

Inset The author's equipment rack on
Moonlight Buttress. *Photo: Andy Kirkpatrick*

The author leading the
final pitch of *Spaceshot*, Zion.
Photo: Andy Kirkpatrick

SOUTH AMERICA

Above Alpamayo: is there anywhere a lovelier Base Camp?

Right Cold morning at Base Camp.

Below Moraine Camp and the view back down the route.

Above Glacier ascent from Moraine Camp. Plenty of 'holes' but nothing threatening.

Right Our team on steeper terrain, nearing the col.

Below The setting sun illuminates Col Camp at the foot of the South-West Face. *Photo: Heather Geluk*

Inset V-thread used for descent. It felt like abseiling off an icicle.

Jaime Avila and the author descending the abseils. *Photo: Chad Peele*

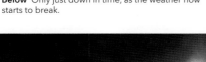

Top right Todd Gessert and Chad Peele descending the Santa Cruz Valley on horseback.

Middle The terrified author. The animal knew what it was doing, but the author didn't. *Photo: unknown*

Bottom right Traditional celebration with support team and their families. Food is baked in the ground.

Below Only just down in time, as the weather now starts to break.

nearby twin peaks of Everest and Lhotse. Both appeared strangely dark and rocky compared with the expanses of unblemished snow immediately around us.

We had made it. Despite the weariness, a huge feeling of satisfaction swept over me. But the wind on the summit was strong and we didn't dawdle there long. We paused for only a moment in the shelter of a shallow depression to eat a nutrition bar and take a drink, then descended the way we had come.

Climbers ritually refer to the summit as the halfway point, and with good reason. More often than not, it's on the way down that the accidents occur. This was probably my most tired-feeling moment of the day, but I forced myself to maintain focus on my rope technique as I arm-wrapped and down-climbed the upper mountain. Wherever possible I elected to abseil, conscious that this was a technique I was more familiar with and which I could reliably execute even when nearing exhaustion. Kharma accompanied me and provided additional security from behind, for which I was very grateful.

We reached Camp 2.7 at 9.15 a.m., having taken an hour and a half to descend what we had climbed that morning. We spent some time organising ourselves and simply resting, which also allowed the others to catch up, keeping the group in touch. Ninety minutes later we were off again. I now felt much stronger and enjoyed the series of arm-wraps and abseils that took us over the Mushroom Ridge and down the Grey Tower. The view over Camp 2 and along the full length of the ridge was even more magnificent in descent. Once again, there was a stark contrast between the copious snow covering the ground at our feet, and the grey, rock-strewn cliffs and moraine that characterised the valleys below, broken only by the distant green-blue tinge of a solitary mountain lake.

We reached Camp 2 at 12.30 and shed our overboots, crampons and much of our outer clothing. Once more we rested, allowing the others to catch up, before setting off again within the hour. We abseiled the Yellow

Tower and worked our way down the ridge to Camp 1, where the Sherpas were already waiting with large bowls of tea.

There remained only the hike to Yak Camp and beyond to the valley bottom. As previously, I reached Base Camp just as the light failed – a little over twelve hours since leaving the tent that morning. It had taken a bit of running to get there, accompanied by an equally enthusiastic Chad. The others weren't far behind and this was the first Alpenglow trip ever on which all the clients returned from the summit to Base Camp in a single day. There was cause to celebrate and soon we were doing exactly that, along with our Sherpas. An evening of beer, wine, whisky – and one of Tashi's signature dishes, roast leg of lamb.

Ahead of us lay a delightful trek, via the monastery at Tengboche, to Namche Bazaar. From there we would retrace our route to Lukla and its airport gateway to Kathmandu. I would enjoy every moment of it. But, for now, I was just happy to go to bed.

When I came next to climb outside my home continent, it was to be a very different type of climb. It all started, though, with another Brit in the UK ...

The *Nose* on El Capitan.

3

NORTH AMERICA

THE NOSE, EL CAPITAN
YOSEMITE
(USA)

I awoke and looked around me. I was lying on a sort of trapeze, suspended horizontally at ninety degrees to a vertical cliff. Cautiously I peered over the edge into the abyss below. It was a somewhat shallow abyss, since the ground lay just ten metres beneath me. My eyes turned to the rock soaring above – all five metres of it. We were on a portaledge, hung on the side of Yarncliffe Quarry in the English Peak District. It did occur to me that no one ever before us had been benighted on a single-pitch British rock climb. But this was no accident. We were rehearsing for another, rather larger, cliff.

The other part of the 'we' was Andy Kirkpatrick, among Britain's top big-wall climbers. The larger cliff was the *Nose* on El Capitan.

Just over a month later I stood with Andy and a third team member, Max Biagosch, at the foot of the sheerest, most featureless granite I had ever seen. El Cap – 'the Captain' as it's often called by locals – rises perpendicular from the ground, astonishingly unblemished by crack or ledge. It's a daunting sight, reminiscent of a modern glass building and equally unyielding to the would-be climber. Alex Honnold, the leading rock climber of the current generation, has called it the most impressive wall on earth.

'Modern aid' climbing was largely created in this valley in Yosemite, and it's easy to see why. The glaciers carved out such vertical, arrow-straight cliffs, with such polished stone, that traditional free climbing was impractical. There simply weren't enough features to allow ascent by purely 'natural' means. New techniques were called for. Nuts, cams, pitons and bolts were no longer required just for insurance should a lead climber fall; they were needed for pulling on to make any upward progress at all. Enter the golden age of the jumar, the etrier (or 'aider' as Americans call them – essentially a sling ladder) and the haul bag, which is needed because of the painfully slow rate of ascent, the huge amount of gear required and the lack of natural water.

That golden age really got under way in the 1950s, and its seminal moment came in November 1958: the conclusion of Warren Harding's forty-five-day conquest of El Capitan by its original route, the *Nose*. That route has become an icon. As the valley guidebook states, 'Long, sustained and flawless, The *Nose* may be the best rock climb in the world; it's certainly the best known', and it remains 'huge, exposed and terrifying'.[14] Who could resist?

El Capitan has two faces joined at sixty degrees by what resembles a ship's prow. Harding's route essentially climbs this prow, although its first four pitches cunningly skirt the immediate verticality by taking a detour off to the left, before returning to the central line at a notable break called Sickle Ledge. This was our objective for the day.

We set off at around 6 a.m. It was virgin ground for all of us. Max was entirely new to Yosemite climbing; I had completed only one significant previous route, the South Face of Washington Column (done the previous year with a local guide, Aaron Jones); and Andy, although this was his twenty-fifth ascent of El Capitan, had never before climbed its most prominent feature, the *Nose*. We were all in a state of awe – in Andy's case with a small 'a', and in Max's and mine with a big 'A' and an exclamation mark!

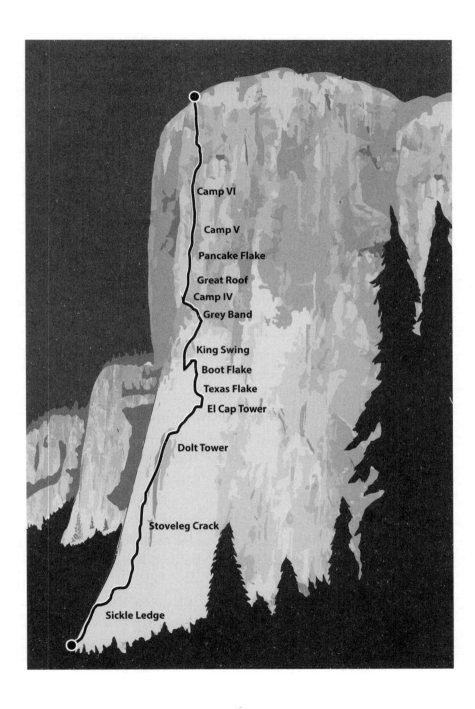

A team of three is ideal for this type of climbing, because there are three distinct roles. The lead climber ascends by placing gear into cracks in the rock and attaching to this his etriers, in which he stands with all his weight. The gear is typically nuts (metal wedges of various kinds) and expanding cams or, more rarely and more challengingly, a simple body-weighted hook (a 'sky hook') placed carefully on a rocky protrusion. This can be supplemented, if necessary, with pitons hammered into the rock, but the modern ethos calls for this practice to be minimised. Where no such cracks or protrusions are available, the leader relies on expansion bolts placed by previous parties, to which a simple karabiner can be clipped. The etriers hang directly from this gear. The lead climber makes upward progress by committing all his weight to one etrier, freeing the other and allowing him to place it higher on the rock. After careful testing, weight is then transferred to this higher etrier, unweighting the lower one and allowing it in turn to be moved higher. In the course of this, the gear is generally recovered for reuse. However, perhaps one in four items of gear is left in situ, as protection, and clipped into the lead rope, which one of the other members of the team belays from below. Much of the time the lead climber is committed to a single piece of gear. Should this fail, he is reliant on the remaining protecting gear and the belay below to arrest his fall. There is often a fair degree of slack in the lead rope – more than would typically be tolerated in free climbing – so when a leader falls, it can be for quite a distance in what is known as a 'whipper'. But serious injuries are rare, because the rock is so sheer that there is nothing sticking out for the falling climber to strike. Although, of course, it can feel like quite a ride down before the rope comes tight.

Once the leader is secure at the belay above, the second team member's responsibility is to jumar up the lead rope, removing all the protecting gear that has been left behind. If the route is straight up, then this is simple, albeit physically demanding. However, if the route traverses left and right, it becomes much more complex. Special techniques are called for, and there is always the risk of an uncontrolled swing.

In addition to the lead rope, the leader drags after him a haul line. This is where the third team member comes into play. He jumars directly up the haul line. This is comparatively straightforward because there is no gear to remove. But, once at the higher belay, this third team member has the somewhat unenviable task of organising the pulley system and hauling up the bag. This is hard enough on a vertical cliff, because the haul bag is typically the weight of a man – about seventy-five kilograms. On a gentler incline the task only becomes harder, due to the additional friction of the bag against the rock. Max and I found that often the best technique was to attach our jumars to the haul line trailing from the pulley, fix the jumars themselves to our harnesses and then hurl ourselves down the face, thus bringing into play our full body weight. This was effective, but had a certain committing feel to it!

In our team, the roles reflected each climber's experience. Andy did all the leading. That meant he provided the brains and the talent and took most of the risk. Max and I followed, cleaning and hauling, which is largely about brawn. Since Max was born in Bavaria and brought up wearing lederhosen, he was well suited to the task. Having been born myself among the dreaming spires of Oxford, where the signature apparel was a straw boater, I was less well prepared. But needs must.

In one sense our initial sortie was a gentle introduction: we had only a very light haul bag, containing just stuff for the day and a gallon of additional water. In another sense these first four pitches provided an early test because they required two tension traverses. Here the leader had to be lowered off and the haul bag belayed out, with the cleaner employing a combination of abseil and jumar in order to follow.

This was all fine while the ropes behaved. But ropes on big walls do not behave, at least not if left to their own devices. Soon we had the mother of all tangles, commonly called a clusterf**k. Then worse: as Max jumared, cleaning the route of the gear that Andy had placed, the rope trailing behind him jammed, caught in some hidden crack. Already tired, he now had to retrace his route down the lead line in order to free it. Half an hour later it happened again. Max looked as though he would cry – only Bavarians don't cry, so it turned into a sort of Teutonic whimper.

Meanwhile, a final swinging traverse on the haul line brought me at last to a position hanging just below Sickle Ledge. An energetic but straightforward jumar and I was up there next to Andy, enjoying the relative comfort of this quite roomy 'eagle's nest'. We congratulated ourselves ... prematurely ...

It was nearing midday and the sun was beating down, generating valley temperatures of up to 38 °C (100 °F). Max was having yet another altercation with the ropes. He lowered out the haul bag only to find he had caught a loop of line around it. A half hour passed as he re-coiled both ropes, all the while in a hanging belay, suspended by his daisy chains (secure leashes). At the end of this laborious process, he looked at us across the expanse of bare rock, murmured 'I'm exhausted', placed his helmeted head in his gloved hands and neither moved nor spoke for fifteen minutes.

This was not good. Andy was filled with alarm. I had known Max for many years and indeed worked alongside him in London. He had spent his life in the mountains and completed many demanding routes, among them the North Face of the Matterhorn. I knew he was anything but a quitter. This collapse seemed very sudden and I was worried that he might be suffering from sunstroke. After what felt like an eternity, Max pulled himself together and climbed slowly over to join us. We were together again. And we were done for the day, at least as far as any upward progress was concerned.

We just needed to get back down to the valley, leaving our fixed lines behind us. This should have been a simple abseil on our two existing ropes plus a third we had stashed in the haul bag, but we managed to turn it into something of an epic. Andy, descending with the additional weight of the bag, fixed the second rope so tightly that Max and I, following, were unable to engage our abseil devices. With the afternoon wind now blowing, communication with Andy was impossible. A huge effort finally secured Max on the line and allowed him to descend. Max in turn was able to create some slack in the rope at the next fixed point and free me from its weight so that I could secure myself and descend too. The whole process took over two hours.

It had been a short day – around eight hours on the rock – but it had not felt easy. Our mood was subdued. We were beginning to understand the magnitude of the challenge presented by this immense wall. If we could make such a meal out of four pitches, how long were the full thirty-one – a kilometre of rock – going to take us? Thankfully, a good dinner lay ahead and a comfortable night in a valley tent.

There followed a day dominated by logistics. In the morning we rested and ate well; bought in all our supplies; packed the haul bag, the porta-ledge and the poop tube; and dragged all three up the fixed lines to Sickle Ledge. Returning to the valley, we rested and ate well (again), before climbing back up to the ledge for the night.

Max and I reached it as the light started to fail. While Andy followed, collecting the ropes, we constructed the portaledge on which Max and I then spent a comfortable night. These portaledges look rather precarious, but offer a naturally ergonomic platform to sleep on. There is the understandable fear of rolling off, but sleepers remain attached by their harness to the main rope, so cannot fall far. Having said that, it would make for quite an awakening, blinking your eyes as you hung suspended in mid-air over an abyss!

Meanwhile, Andy laid out his mat on the flattest available rock. We all slept pretty well until we were woken at 4.20 a.m. by the sound of violent thunder. Only it wasn't thunder. It was rockfall. Huge rockfall. To the east of us, a large chunk of El Cap had plummeted into the valley, leaving a white scar on the cliff and a vast cloud of granite dust that hung in the air like morning mist. It was a sobering sight.

A couple of hours after that, we were away. The first two pitches were undemanding and we ran them into one. In the course of this I acquired a third, previously abandoned, rope that Andy asked me to bring along too. We now had three eighty-metre ropes to deal with.

The next two pitches proved a major test, possibly *the* major test of the whole climb. Both were rightward traverses. On the first, Max lowered out Andy, who clawed his way over and slightly down under tension from above, before then climbing upwards to a higher belay called Dolt Hole. Next, I lowered Max out on the haul line. He was thus belayed from above and below. Once suspended directly beneath the new belay, he could easily jumar up to it. The haul bag followed. That left me to jumar up the lead rope. Clearly, though, I also needed some means of countering the swing. To achieve this, I trailed the end of the lead rope behind me, fed this through a mallion (solid metal ring) at the belay and lowered myself off using my GriGri, an assisted-braking belay device.

I joined Max at Dolt Hole tired, thirsty and hungry. Andy had moved on and was already out of earshot due to a thunderous, tornado-like wind that seemed at its most violent at this point. The stance was another hanging one, with 250 metres of clean drop below. The inability to communicate, the precipitous nature of the rock, the sense of vulnerability engendered by the hanging stance, and the reliance on a couple of bolts to hold the three of us plus the haul bag, all conspired to create a feeling of exposure I was not prepared for. Furthermore, there were now three ropes streaming out below me and disappearing from view, tossed by the wind to snag on who knew what. And, of course, those ropes were tangled. I was stressed.

On reflection, I don't think there is anything that quite compares with the sense of exposure on El Capitan – nothing I have experienced, anyway. The wall is so absolute, so uncompromising. Many non-climbers claim they have a special fear of heights: vertigo or something similar.

But experienced climbers feel this fear, too. If they didn't, they'd probably be dead. We all, to one degree or another, become uncomfortable, at least initially, when suspended over emptiness. And we all have a need to acclimate to this, to build our confidence in whatever is securing us. It takes some time to get used to. On this occasion, it took me quite a lot of time. It never even occurred to me to quit, but I did question whether I was really up to it. I was intimidated, narrowly focused on my own survival and, as a result, of little help to my partners.

I paused for a moment, knowing that I must simplify the situation. During a brief respite in the wind, I managed to communicate with Andy. We agreed to ditch the third rope. I released it and watched it snake down into the valley. It sounds like a small thing, but this freed just enough mental bandwidth for me to start getting back on top of things. Challenges remained, yet it was at least the beginning of something better.

Following Andy and Max required another rightwards traverse. Again, I lowered myself out, but this time attempted simultaneously to jumar on the rope above me. A mistake. These techniques should be used in turn, not together. Now I really did hear Andy. He screamed from above, 'Both hands on the GriGri!' I corrected the mistake, completed the horizontal traverse and only then jumared up to the belay, where at last Andy, Max and I were reunited. I was learning, albeit the hard way.

Andy and Max had clearly been having a serious conversation. Andy had asked Max whether he wanted to go down. Max had replied, 'No.' I felt the same. But it was clear that Andy's confidence in us was being tested. Meanwhile, it seemed that all those around us were bailing. A pair from above abseiled past us, headed down, while another pair, who had caught up from below, promptly turned tail too. The wind remained very strong and the sense of exposure was still almost overpowering.

However, I was past the worst and the way ahead looked easier. We were now in the celebrated Stoveleg Crack, where Harding and his team leapfrogged their way up using four pitons forged from the legs of an old stove. The crack looked demanding, but at least it was straight up all the way to a sizeable bivvy that was our destination for the night.

A vital step towards regaining control was mastering the ropes. Ditching the third one had helped. Two other things further improved the situation: first, stashing the ropes properly in the rope bags that we carried with us, rather than having them trailing below us, getting ever more tangled with each other; and second, recognising that we had two ends to the haul line, one attached to me and one to the haul bag, both of which if necessary could be untied and thus permit untangling. From that moment on, we had plenty of 'clusterf**ks' but none that we were unable to resolve before the ropes came tight. The 'we' in this was important, because the other crucial element was teamwork. Max and I both calmed down sufficiently to be able to look beyond our own immediate task and security and work to help each other. Together we were much more effective.

At the ninth belay, halfway up the Stoveleg, we regrouped again in better spirits. The wind was dropping. The ropes were tangled once more, but this time Max and I sorted them out efficiently. Andy, leading off, was able to proceed unhindered. The rest of the crack and a final short corner went without incident, delivering us on to the sizeable ledge of Dolt Tower at 6.30 p.m.

This gave us sensible, even luxurious, time to organise a bivouac, with two and a half hours of light remaining. We made the most of it. Up went the portaledge. Out came our rations: a supper of bagels with tuna and cream cheese, washed down with an energy drink. And out there was a very special view. The wall dropped directly below us to a tree-covered valley floor, which spread as far as the granite walls on the opposite side of the gorge. It is important to remember that the Yosemite Valley has more in common with the Grand Canyon than with the Alps. El Capitan does not so much rise up from the valley as dive down into it; it's more canyon wall than mountain face.

Despite our apparent solitude, we were not entirely alone. Below we could hear the calls of two British climbers still making their way up Stoveleg Crack. And here I learnt something about Andy. Andy is a very smart man. And I don't mean just street-smart; he is super-smart. He is insatiably curious – about everything. A conversation with Andy can sometimes feel like a benign interrogation. The combination of this intellectual power with a character that's extraordinarily resilient – the traditional climbing term is 'hard' – in my view explains why Andy is such a strong big-wall climber. Big walls are jokingly referred to as 'blue-collar' climbing because so much hard manual work is involved in jumaring, hauling and just surviving. But they also require real intellect. They are a puzzle that must be unlocked. It's less about gymnastics and more about engineering.

On Dolt Tower I saw that Andy is also a remarkably selfless person. Max and I had the portaledge. That left plenty of room on flat ground for Andy, since Dolt Tower has bivvy space for two. Yet Andy chose instead to sleep on a miserable pile of uneven blocks, leaving the flat ground for the two British climbers who were still fighting their way through the night. I know few, if any, climbers who would have done this. The accepted rule at bivvies is first come, first served. The British pair didn't make it to the ledge until 5 a.m., but still the gesture said a lot about Andy.

The night was not complete without a bit of drama. As we sat in our sleeping bags gazing out at our moonlit mountain panorama, over our heads fell a body … and then another. Both passed with a strange whirring sound, black shadows in the night. A pair of climbers had fallen from above – but not by accident. As they neared the ground, small white canopies opened and cars waiting below switched on their headlights. These were base jumpers. They jump in the dark because it's illegal to do so in the national park, which is under federal rather than state jurisdiction.

Such illicit pursuits raise the other great question that sits alongside 'Why do people participate in high-risk activities?' – that is, 'Should they be *allowed* to participate in them?' This latter debate has concerned itself with everything from wearing motorcycle helmets to base jumping to, of course, climbing itself. Frequent have been the calls for a ban on climbs as various as Everest, Mont Blanc and El Cap, and they are usually triggered by an accident of one kind or another.

The main current of western contemporary thinking on this subject has taken its lead from John Stuart Mill. In a celebrated passage from his 1859 essay *On Liberty*, Mill asserts his central principle: 'the only purpose for which power can be rightfully exercised over any member of a civilised community, against his will, is to prevent harm to others.'[15] This has left those seeking to prohibit activities such as climbing flailing around for reasons why it harms non-participants. Some cite the demands that such pursuits place on rescue teams and the health service. But if this were the real concern, then the measured response would not be a complete ban, but rather some form of compulsory insurance. A further argument highlights the distress caused to those who witness such accidents and to the family and friends of those injured, but that seems a somewhat marginal argument and could equally apply to a ban on alcohol or automobiles. Do we really want to go back to Prohibition and the horse-drawn cart?

A few have argued against Mill that society does have an obligation to protect the individual from himself. This position is not entirely without philosophical foundation. The late Derek Parfit, in his contrarian and thought-provoking work *Reasons and Persons*, claimed that our young selves often differ from our old selves more than we differ from each other – in attitude, preferences, tolerance of risk and so on – and that we are therefore, in a sense, multiple persons over our lifetime. On that basis one might contend that society has an obligation to prevent our young selves from harming our old-selves-to-be by throwing away our future lives in the reckless pursuit of risk. It's an argument, but it has never struck me as a compelling one. It rings too much of the tyranny of the old over the young. So, I'm with Mill. If I choose to climb, that's up to me. And if those base jumpers choose to take to the sky, well, that too is up to them. With such self-justifying thoughts, I happily dozed off, and slept rather well.

We were up with the light. Huddled next to us were the forlorn, exhausted bodies of the British pair, John and David. We tried not to disturb them, but that wasn't easy as we dragged the haul bag across the ledge.

Another traverse right required Andy to be lowered off into a crack system so he could resume upward progress and then return left, again rolling two pitches into one. I in turn lowered Max out, who jumared the haul line and then set about pulling up the haul bag, with the portaledge and poop tube attached. Finally, I bade farewell to my tired compatriots and lowered myself off the ledge, which was made easier by a fixed line trailing from the bivvy site. There were no hiccups. We were finally getting the hang of this. One further, uneventful pitch brought us to El Cap Tower, a roomy ledge with space for six. Andy had floated this as a possible objective for the day, but we were now humming, and there was no serious question of stopping there.

Next came the Texas Flake, a huge upright chunk of rock with a gap behind it that separated it from the rest of the cliff. Andy, as leader, had to climb this narrow gap, bridging between flake and mountain, feet on one, back to the other. Only it wasn't as narrow as he would have liked. Either that or his body wasn't as long as he would have liked. Anyway, his verdict was, 'SCARY!' We dutifully followed to a belay on the top of the flake, perilously balanced with a drop on either side. Flakes were the order of the day: the following pitch was the Boot Flake, a remarkable boot-shaped feature that the Duke of Wellington would have been proud of.

And having surmounted that, we were at last positioned for one of those great moments in a climbing lifetime: the King Swing. How Warren Harding figured this out in 1958 beats me. Yet he knew he needed to complete a big traverse back left, and reckoned the only way that could be done was with a massive pendulum. Since we were following in his footsteps, that's the way we went, too. Max lowered Andy down half a length of rope. From there Andy moved initially right, to build momentum, before swinging back left in a huge arc, bounding across the rock with his feet and clawing with his hands for a suitable hold to prevent him returning whence he'd come. It took Harding five swings to find the hold he was looking for at the left extremity of the pendulum, and it took Andy much the same. But he made it, to a chorus of shouts from those watching through telescopes down in the valley. From there a crack system led up to a belay at similar height to ours.

It was Max's turn. Near disaster followed. Max had inadvertently attached his jumars upside down and failed to employ his GriGri. Facing downwards, the jumars are prone to detach. And without a backup belay device, Max had no second line of defence. He would have fallen to his death. Halfway across the traverse Andy realised the twin errors. Later he admitted his instinct was to cry out, but instead he calmly … very calmly … asked Max to attach the GriGri and then reverse the jumars. A close call.

Next I lowered off the haul bag, and lastly myself, running my trailing rope through an available mallion. Despite the near miss, we had completed one of the major obstacles of the *Nose* with great efficiency.

The eighteenth pitch included another pendulum. This time I had some fun, imitating Andy by skipping across the rock in huge leaping strides to catch a loop of rope thrown by Max. In contrast to the great king-sized original, Andy mockingly dubbed my effort 'Charles's Princess Swing'. A significant change had occurred. We were now thoroughly enjoying this climb. Fear and intimidation had given way to respect, but also fun.

Halfway across the nineteenth pitch, in the so-called Grey Band, we decided to make camp for the night. This was to be the most spectacular bivouac of them all. The portaledge was suspended against the perfectly sheer wall, rather like a VIP box at the opera, jutting over the stage. It was the proverbial view to die for – although I was increasingly of the view that we weren't actually going to die. The setting sun caught the cliffs opposite, bathing them in that warm glow that comes particularly at the end of the day. Now that we were so much higher, the trees in the valley appeared like the toy foliage used by architects to enliven their model constructions. There was an unreal feeling about the whole thing. As we gazed into the valley over dinner, the rising moon and another base jumper together provided *son et lumière* entertainment. Our confidence in achieving our goal was growing. Spirits were high.

We awoke well rested, and munched the remainder of our muesli while trying not to think about the date: Friday 13th. Leaving the haul bag on a ledge, we took an easy traverse left to what is called Camp IV, and from there climbed to a stance overhung by the *Nose*'s best-known feature, the Great Roof. Harding had expected this to be the crux of his climb, but in fact had tamed it with relative ease. We would make similarly light work of it. Yet the majesty of the Great Roof remained. It was spectacular. Andy followed the crack line beneath the roof, which had lots of abandoned tat to aid his way. There was one demanding long reach right, but with that overcome, he comfortably made it to an airy stance beyond the huge overhang.

The Kirkpatrick brain had figured out that between the haul rope and the surplus lead rope, we had enough to drag our haul bag from its ledge at our last bivouac all the way to the top of the Great Roof in one super-efficient lift. And that's what we did. The British pair behind subsequently tried the same, resulting in a jammed haul bag and an epic effort to free it. Why the different outcomes? I have no idea. There is art and mystery as well as science in this work.

Two further pitches, including the Pancake Flake, brought us to a sort of pulpit, Camp V; and another two, up a very straight chimney system, to the imaginatively named Camp VI. This, our fourth bivvy, was a reasonable ledge, but jammed into a somewhat darkened corner. Max and I again took the portaledge while Andy lay on a rock ledge beneath. Wedged tight into his cramped billet, Andy reflected, 'I think I'm an indoor person.' Wonderful, coming from the author of *Psychovertical* and *Cold Wars*.

Life on a portaledge is not an entirely easy one. For a start everything must be attached: mattress, bivvy bag, sleeping bag, water bottle, pee bottle, headlamp, shoes, gloves, spare clothing … Anything that isn't attached is likely to be lost and might well be a danger to those below. But, once familiar, the portaledge is actually quite comfortable, and I certainly slept well. Rather better than Andy did!

Come the morning, Max and I were struggling to contain our excitement. Only five pitches remained. We knew we could expect to top out that day. There were two more straight pitches before the route veered a little right under another, smaller roof. Coming up cleaning behind, I was delighted to find my technique now much more proficient. 'About time', one might reasonably say. Anyway, the proper combination of GriGri and jumars allowed me to progress rapidly, extracting all the gear as I went. Soon I joined Andy and Max at the thirtieth belay with just a single pitch left to climb.

This final pitch is the subject of one of the best-loved stories in Yosemite folklore. Warren Harding climbed through the entire night, placing by the light of his head torch a seemingly endless line of bolts. Come the morning, having scaled a spectacular overhang, the *Nose*'s last defence, he emerged to the embrace of friends and media, a hero of his times.

In a gesture of great generosity, Andy now passed over the lead to me for this magnificent finale. The first two-thirds was a bolt ladder with just one piece of traditional gear to place. I revelled in it, knowing myself secure, but enjoying the sensational exposure and the sheer gymnastic thrill. Beyond this, the final third of the pitch was free climbing, but on gently sloping slabs that I padded up with ease. And there I was, all of a sudden, at the top of El Capitan, having completed surely the greatest rock climb in the world.

Topping out like this was actually quite disorienting. The transition from the world of the vertical to the world of the horizontal was so total and so immediate. Because its geology is more canyon than mountain, the top of El Cap is not a spiky summit of the alpine kind, but rather an extensive level plain of sandy ground, broken by occasional rocks, extensive undergrowth, and mature trees with impressively oversized fir cones. After five days on the wall, I now found myself visually confused, almost dizzy. Here I could walk around, sit down, take off my helmet and place it carelessly on the ground without securing it in any fashion. It took a while to adjust.

Soon Max and Andy were at my side. We found the traditional tree and hugged it ritually; then hugged each other. It was a special moment. And it was a moment we wanted to last, to savour just for a while, so rather than rush back to the valley, we camped up there on the top of El Cap for one final night.

We now had an uninterrupted view down the valley. The setting sun cast a warm red glow over the giant cliff face and rounded shoulder of the Half Dome. Just as El Cap dominates the west end of the Yosemite Valley, so the Half Dome makes its claim on the east.

One man who didn't welcome Harding's success on the *Nose*, or, if he did, only through gritted teeth, was Royal Robbins. The two climbers were the towering figures in the valley, and not only of their own generation – of all generations. But they were markedly different characters: Harding the irreverent carefree playboy; Robbins the meticulously careful, disciplined planner. Robbins made the greatest-but-one conquest in the valley, the North-West Face of the Half Dome, in 1957, but the greatest of all was denied him just a year later by Harding, in his eyes the undeserving prodigal brother. A pain perhaps too much to bear: Robbins was driven at one point to sawing off the bolts previously placed by his rival. Later he regretted this, but it's doubtful he ever overcame the disappointment of being beaten to 'the Captain'.

We awoke one last time on El Cap. As we ate breakfast, a deer grazed next to our campsite. There was a deep feeling of peace. A long walk to the valley lay ahead of us, but it would be a happy one. And those other two British climbers, John and David, made it too. We all had pizza and beer together down in the valley.

But the climbing was not yet over. I had not set myself the 'seven routes' challenge as a tick-box exercise: seven tasks to be completed and then never revisited. These climbs were an opportunity to try something new, somewhere different. And so for me, the climb on the *Nose* was not an ending but a beginning. That final pitch had given me a feel for what leading on aid was like. It fascinated me and terrified me at the same time. I knew I had to do more.

Before leaving Yosemite, I led four pitches on the *Leaning Tower*, a Royal Robbins classic and supposedly the steepest climb in North America (it leans the wrong way!). It was a rapid education in life at the sharp end of the rope, especially when I slipped off a sky hook and took a twenty-foot whipper. The following year I returned to El Capitan with Andy for another six-day ascent, but this time by a route called *Zodiac*, more technical and steeper than the *Nose*. Memorably, a plastic water bottle accidentally dropped on the fifth day fell clean to the valley floor without once touching the rock. This time Andy allowed me to lead most of the climb: eleven of the sixteen pitches. It was a fight with fear all the way, but like a drug addict I only seemed to want more. So, a further trip followed, this time to Zion in Utah, where I led *Moonlight Buttress* and seconded Andy on *Spaceshot*. Such majestic routes give new meaning to the word privilege. But, the beginning of it all for me was Warren Harding's inspired vision, the *Nose* on El Capitan.

The next two of the seven routes would each involve an element of looking back as well as looking forward. They would evoke memories of younger years, adding a new spice to the endeavour.

South-West Face of Alpamayo.

SOUTH AMERICA

SOUTH-WEST FACE OF ALPAMAYO
CORDILLERA BLANCA
(PERU)

I was hanging by the rope, suspended in a large, cold, icy crevasse. Its name, Garganta, Spanish for 'throat', seemed uncomfortably appropriate. Flailing away with two ice tools, I had missed the sling that our local guide Vicenti had placed to help us across. A silly mistake, but perhaps an understandable one in the pitch dark and speaking few words of Spanish beyond *cerveza*. Nor did it help being weakened by illness, frostbite and two nights trapped by a blizzard in a collapsing tent at 6,100 metres.

My partner Ted and I were both twenty years old and had little climbing experience beyond North Wales and the British Lake District. Vicenti had first scoffed at the idea of taking us up, then cried with fear (literally) and then agreed. The truth was he'd had little choice. He'd been told to take us by the local 'fixer', whose nickname – Pepe El Loco – spoke a thousand words. This was not a situation my mother would have approved of. But these were the days before mobile phones and the internet, and she had no idea we were even climbing. After all, we'd set off from home with nothing more than a couple of pairs of firm hiking boots. One volcano had sort of led to another and now we were on a proper mountain, in fact the highest mountain in the Peruvian Andes and the fourth highest in the western hemisphere.

I pulled myself together, metaphorically and physically, clawed my way back on to the icy ridge whence I'd come, and tried again. This time I found the sling with one hand, as I thrust in hard with the front points of both crampons into the opposing wall of the crevasse, and then wielded my ice axe with the other arm, casting it in a long arc that buried the pick in the snow on the far side. Still half-frozen in the chill of the pre-dawn, the snow was firm enough. The axe held. Success. I was over.

A lot of hard ice work followed. And some real excitement when, on a steep traverse, both my ill-fitting borrowed crampons detached from my equally ill-fitting borrowed boots. Then a tricky move to circumvent a rocky outcrop brought us to a small ledge and a steeper ice wall. Vicenti cut steps up to another plateau. More steep ice, but then at last easier ground – at least, as easy as it can feel when the air is so thin that you're taking two breaths for every step.

The bad weather was getting worse. I felt I could go no further. Ted was equally desperate. We were exhausted. Out of the mist and the murk appeared a faint hint of red … which became a fluttering of red … and at last a clearly visible red flag. We were at 6,768 metres and had reached the summit of Huascarán.

We had fulfilled an absurd ambition. But a second had been fuelled. While we had planned and climbed this route, we had heard repeatedly of another mountain close by, one with an extraordinary ice face that none who saw it could ever forget: a mountain by the name of Alpamayo.

Thirty-four years later …

It was now July 2014 and I was back in the Huascarán National Park. I woke in a grassy meadow with the sound of gurgling streams nearby, and struggled out of my tent into the beautiful morning. The sun had not yet struck the tents, but its full force illuminated the ice-clad mountains above: Artesonraju, Quitaraju and, queen of them all, Alpamayo. Even from this side – not its finest profile – Alpamayo was captivating in the early dawn. It was the perfect backdrop for breakfast outside: scrambled eggs, bacon, fried potatoes and toast with fresh-ground coffee, prepared by our local Peruvian cook, Alfredo.

This was now our team's eighth day in Peru. We had been on a journey from the decidedly miserable, through the increasingly fun and interesting, to the truly sublime. The decidedly miserable starting point had been Lima. I had visited this metropolis twice previously and felt no need to rush back for more. Once (or less) would have sufficed. Sadly, Lima has all the problems one associates with the capital cities of most developing countries, and few of the redeeming features. On this trip we had stayed in one of its smartest neighbourhoods, Miraflores, the home of many of the city's foreign embassies. It could, at best, be described as boring. This is not to castigate all Peru's cities. The country's second largest, Arequipa, is enriched with attractive colonial architecture from the period of Spanish occupation. And there are many smaller towns with open squares and colourful bustling streets.

One such is Huaraz (3,052 metres), the largest town in the country's highest mountain range, the Cordillera Blanca. Our bus journey there from Lima had taken nine hours and involved an ascent of four vertical kilometres and then a drop of one. We had left behind the barren landscape of the coastal desert plain for the verdant, even luxurious, vegetation of the mountain valleys, rock faces soaring skyward on every side. In this northern enclave we had checked into a delightful family-run hotel, breakfasted on its rooftop, mountain-biked in the nearby hills for acclimatisation, strolled in the town's streets in the bracing cool of the evening air, and drunk rather more Pisco Sours than were strictly good for us.

A further three-hour drive along dirt roads with precipitous drops and distant views of Huascarán – for me distant in time as well as place – had brought us to the tiny village of Cashapampa. There, at the mouth of an impressive gorge, we had hired a team of *burros* and their drivers to carry our baggage. And up we had gone, ascending steeply alongside a river punctuated by waterfalls and flanked by flowers. Over the following days, we had enjoyed the trek up this now-famous valley, the Santa Cruz, with its extraordinary mix of mountain meadow, tranquil lake and flat alluvial sand. Eventually we had broken off left into a smaller valley and enjoyed the cool shade of an almost primeval-feeling wooded landscape, before zigzagging up to find ourselves at one of the most pristine and picturesque campsites I have ever encountered (4,330 metres). This was Base Camp.

And so, at last, we were in position to mount a proper assault on our objective. Alpamayo is one of the more remote peaks within the Cordillera Blanca. Indeed, it famously failed to appear at all on a map of 1932, and was not climbed by any route until 1957, four years after Everest.

We spent the morning preparing for our departure. The climbing team numbered six. Chad (forty) was our American guide, with whom I had climbed previously in Nepal. He led off shortly after midday with me (the oldest at fifty-four) and a fellow Brit, Alasdair (the youngest at sixteen). Jaime (forty-seven), our Ecuadorian guide, followed with another American, Todd (forty), and Heather (thirty-eight), a joint Canadian and Dutch national who lived in London. It was an international team for sure, and one that spanned the generations. On the support side, in addition to Alfredo, we had two able helpers in the unfailingly upbeat Pablo and Julio.

Adjusting to altitude is always a rather personal thing and, in this particular case, it was the oldest and the youngest who were adapting fastest. So, I strode along with Alasdair, still a teenager and a year younger than my own youngest child. He displayed a maturity beyond his years, his true age revealed only in an occasional tendency to race on, overcome by a need to see what lay ahead. He was a delightful companion, full of enthusiasm. He also promised to be an asset when it came to the ice climbing ahead, having completed a number of steep routes in Canada.

The ascent from 4,340 metres to the Moraine Camp at 4,950 metres took little more than an hour and a half. It began with trees, streams and flowers, moved through burnt earth and scrub, and ended with bare rock and scree. Barren though the new camp looked, it offered flat ground, running water and a view over the turquoise Lake Arhueycocha to the sand-filled plain, and beyond that the verdant pastures of the Santa Cruz Valley.

Having dropped a cache of hardware at the foot of the glacier (5,000 metres), we enjoyed a last supper al Alfredo and admired the rising of the full moon before turning in for the night.

We roused as the first rays of sun hit the tent, and set off at 9.30 a.m. heavily laden – albeit less burdened than we would have been without the porterage skills of Pablo and Julio. We were soon ascending the glacier, on two ropes of three, togged up in crampons and helmets and with ice axes in hand. It was a benign glacier, offering a pleasant gradient, meandering line, scenery sculpted by deep crevasses and distant hanging séracs (cliffs of ice) – and yet almost no real danger. It never felt as though anything would fall on top of us, nor that the world would disappear beneath our feet.

The route trended slightly right before traversing horizontally back a long way left. Chad, Alasdair and I had drawn some distance ahead, and on this more level ground we waited to allow the other three to catch up. It was a long wait. They were moving slowly.

When they arrived, there was a discussion between Todd and the two guides. Todd was clearly a capable mountaineer, having climbed extensively in the Cascades, Alaska, Ecuador and Nepal. But he had been sick from the first day, the result of food poisoning in Huaraz. This and the resulting sleepless nights had taken their toll on an otherwise superbly fit guy. He was very weak. After some thought, he took the brave but painful decision to retreat. I guess, as an experienced Delta Airlines pilot, Todd knew better than to take himself into such a challenging environment in anything less than full health. The clients were now down to three.

While Jaime descended with Todd, we others continued upward. Not for long, though. Soon we reached a more threatening passage that was fine for a roped party to cross, but risky for a single climber. We waited again to allow Jaime to join us. Reunited, we progressed on two ropes, soon collecting a third, comprising Pablo and Julio. The route moved into the shadow and steepened. We stopped to put on more clothing and retrieve our second ice tools. The way now went straight up, traversed right along a narrow ridge, then crossed an area of broken ground, wind-blown snow and deep holes before ascending steeply to the col. This required our first front-pointing with crampons and full swinging placements with both ice tools. Chad secured us with some fixed protection and a snow stake, so we were in no real danger, although there was a feeling of exposure as we teetered above the open crevasse.

At 2.15 p.m. we reached the col (5,600 metres), direct sunshine and a view that silenced us all. I had seen many a photograph and read half a dozen first-hand accounts, but none of this had quite prepared me for that first moment gazing across at the South-West Face of Alpamayo. I was star-struck. With not a rock or blemish, it is marked only by icy striations: long flutes of blue and white, separated by glistening ridges. An uncompromising wall of ice, rising apparently vertically from the glacier to the skyline. It's no surprise that in 1966, readers of the German climbing magazine *Alpinismus* voted Alpamayo the most beautiful mountain in the world.

Viewed from our col, the mountain's highest point seemed indisputable. However, those who first attempted its ascent did so by the north ridge, the one furthest from where we stood. From their vantage point it was anything but certain, the summit ridge appearing more like the teeth of an upturned saw blade, with real doubt as to which tooth stood highest.

First to try was a Swiss party of three in 1948. They climbed the ridge to within view of the top, only to have a cornice (an icy overhang, sculpted

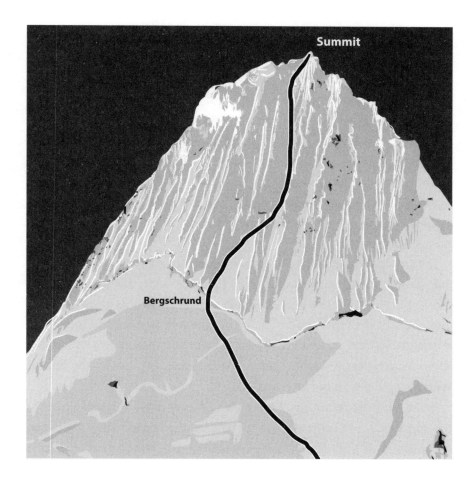

by the wind) break beneath them and cast them into the void. By some miracle they survived the 200-metre fall, but understandably enough was enough. In the words of the *Alpine Journal*, Alpamayo had repulsed its first suitor.

A Franco–Belgian team followed three years later. They avoided the cornices by detouring on to the east face (hidden from our view). They made it on to the 'saw tooth' ridge and announced in their subsequent account that 'at last our dreams had come true and Alpamayo lay conquered at our feet'[16] ... but the mountain had deceived them. The team were still some seventy metres below the true summit, and more than twice that distance in horizontal terms. And the shortfall was of no little consequence: the remaining ridge presented many obstacles for those who followed.

The real conquerors came in the form of a German team in 1957. They eschewed the northern approach in favour of the south ridge, which lay now at *our* feet. Though no less demanding, this route had the significant advantage of reaching the summit ridge much closer to its highest point which, they said, 'pierced the skyline like the prow of some great Viking ship.'[17]

The troubled north ridge eventually succumbed to a British team in 1966. They, however, pointed to the challenge that still remained, the greatest of them all: the South-West Face – in the words of one of their number, 'a perfect trapezoid of fluted ice, incredibly steep and seemingly impregnable from all angles.'[18] This aspect of the mountain would repel attempts on it for a further decade. And it was this aspect, the South-West Face, that we aimed to climb.

Again our team regrouped before I led the way down the easy slopes to the so-called Col Camp at 5,450 metres, on the broad plateau between Alpamayo and Quitaraju. There we settled into four tents and made ourselves at home. I shared a tent with Alasdair. Heather had a tent to herself and made the most of it.

Heather had clearly perfected the art of being comfortable. I say this not in mockery, but in true admiration. Heather was a wonderful contradiction. A semi-professional climber and ambassador for Sherpa outdoor clothing who boxed three times a week, she nonetheless described herself as a diva and lover of pink nail polish. Even after a week in a tent without a shower, which had left the rest of us looking like escaped inmates from a particularly unsavoury penal institution, Heather's blond hair appeared as if straight out of the salon. She firmly subscribed to the mantra that 'Any fool can rough it'. The challenge was to be comfortable even in testing conditions. And she was. Inevitably this prompted some unwarranted teasing from her male colleagues, who nicknamed her 'HM', for 'High Maintenance', all of which she took with very good humour. The truth is we were just envious.

Along with us, there was one other team made up of two Peruvian guides, two American clients and two local porters. Like us, they planned to attempt the Face early the following morning.

I was already fully dressed in my sleeping bag as the designated hour approached. Wearing three thermal under-layers, heavy trousers, wind jacket, full 6,000-metre duvet jacket plus woolly hat, I was barely warm. It was 2.30 a.m. and a howling wind was buffeting the tent. Chad and Jaime consulted and concluded that we should delay our summit bid until the following day. Back to bed.

We eventually crawled out of our tents at 10 a.m. On the horizon were lenticular clouds, often indicative of strong winds and poor weather. Closer to hand, though, were the fluffy white variety – far less threatening. The weather was hard to read. There was little to do but wait. Meanwhile, we watched the other team inch painfully slowly up the face. One pair made it; the other gave up well before the summit. It was 3.30 p.m. when they regained the camp, fourteen hours after departing. We were glad to have waited.

A short excursion over towards Quitaraju helped stretch our legs, but our minds were fixed on Alpamayo. Would we get the weather to attempt the summit? And if we did, would we reach it? Late in the afternoon, two more teams arrived, each with one guide and one client.

There was further wind in the night, but it dropped in the early hours. By 3.30 a.m. it was calm, with just a little cloud, which meant welcome warmer temperatures. We were on. We ascended the gentle incline up to the bergschrund, the large crevasse that marks the chaotic join of ice face and glacier, and climbed into it, just left of the main line where it was filled with snow and icy rubble. There we prepared for the two-tooled, pitched climbing above.

Our target was a route that threads its way straight up from the bergschrund and tops out right at the summit. The original route on the Face was put up by an Italian team in 1975. Five years later, an American duo attempted to emulate them, but lost their way and unintentionally opened up a much more direct route. Despite the Americans' pioneering efforts, their route is now called the French Direct, taking its name rather darkly from the attempted third ascent, when a French pair were killed by a collapsing ice tower. That's where we were headed.

There in the bergschrund, the stillness of the pre-dawn was broken by a lone voice saying, 'I feel ill.' It came from Alasdair, who sat slumped in the dark on a mound of snow. Our headlamps all swung around to pinpoint him, like a night scene from *The Great Escape*. Jaime made a closer inspection. Alasdair's pupils appeared dilated.

Chad delivered a volley of questions: 'What is your surname? What mountain are you on? What year is it?' Alasdair answered them all correctly but in a slow, laboured fashion. It didn't feel at all good. His summit day was over. Chad roped up with Alasdair and together they retreated to the tents. Three had become two.

Heather seemed shaken by what had occurred. She was convinced she wouldn't manage the seven pitches above, and told me so. She seemed deeply concerned that, were she to turn back higher up the Face, then she would also force my retreat. It was a selfless thought. I didn't know what to say – all I could offer was something inane like, 'Why not take it one pitch at a time?'

Jaime had now long disappeared, rightwards around the corner, on to the Face proper and up to the first belay. Heather followed. She thrust out with both tools, wielding them in an arc above her head, competently negotiating the remaining bergschrund and establishing herself on the open snow slope that formed the lower part of the flute.

From there the sensible thing would have been for her to bring her ice tools down to waist level and use a sort of dagger technique. The snow in the flute was relatively soft. Lowering the tools would have allowed blood to flow back into her arms, an important consideration when it was still early in the day, dark and cold. However, Heather continued upwards still arcing her tools. Soon she was complaining of cold hands. I came up close behind on an independent rope and encouraged her to change her technique. But she was now in the zone, one familiar to most of us, where attention becomes so focused that it's akin to tunnel vision. She seemed unable to take in what I was saying. I set the issue aside, planning to raise it again at the belay.

At the belay, though, Heather was close to panic. Having lost feeling in her hands, she felt that she must get down immediately. I tied her into the belay with a clove hitch and tried to reassure her. The sun would be up in an hour and bring with it warmer temperatures. But she would not reconsider. Jaime lowered us both off and down-climbed himself. We were back at the bergschrund. Heather had regained her composure as quickly as she had lost it. She insisted that she would be fine making her own way back to the tents. She was clearly determined not to deprive me of a chance at the summit. Even under such stress, she still wanted to put others first. I was touched but saddened to lose her. Jaime lowered Heather to safe ground. Two was now one.

Despite Heather's selfless gesture, Jaime was for calling off the whole climb and trying again the next day. It was 6.15 a.m. and late to be starting out afresh. But I argued that the time we set out was unimportant. What mattered was the time we expected to get back. I was confident that, working efficiently as a pair, the two of us would be back at the tents at an earlier hour than the five of us could ever have hoped to be. Jaime took the point. We strapped on our packs, switched off our now-redundant headlamps, took hold of our ice tools, and up we went.

The first three pitches were of a similar character: straight up fifty-five-degree *névé*, which was soft enough to climb almost entirely with ice tools used dagger-fashion. Jaime, already familiar with the route, was happy to push on with only that protection left by previous parties, supplemented by a couple of snow stakes. I was feeling strong and fairly raced up behind him. I didn't want him to change his mind!

The two pairs who had arrived the previous day were now ahead of us. This created a certain added interest. Given the direct nature of the route, Jaime and I, as the third pair, were in the firing line. While belaying, I inevitably had three climbers moving above me, all hacking away with their axes and sending down debris that ranged from harmless powder to dinner-plate-sized lumps of rock-hard ice. Never was a helmet more called for. Mine took a lot of impact. Looking up to see how everybody was doing was a rash act; taking photos rasher still.

However, our speed meant that we were soon climbing parallel with the nearer of the two pairs, who were making rather ponderous progress using jumars on a fixed line. Another couple of pitches and we were ahead. Things improved still further as the other leading pair began their descent and moved below us. We were now the highest on the Face. At last we were the ones raining havoc, rather than the ones being rained on!

Meanwhile the character of the slope had changed. The route was steepening and the accommodating *névé* had turned to hard ice. Here the technique was rather more of the 'fly on the wall' variety, with axes swinging overhead and front points of crampons carrying the body weight. Such conditions called for greater security, and Jaime placed his first ice screw.

The route trended up and slightly right before again straightening into a narrow gully. The pitch here was seventy degrees, just twenty degrees off the vertical. A ridge of hard ice split the path ahead, presenting a choice between two runnels, each shoulder-width. On the left was soft, but steep, unconsolidated snow; on the right was bullet-hard ice. I made the wrong choice, went left and was soon swimming in powdery snow that just wouldn't bear my weight. I floundered around and eventually clawed my way right to the comparative security of the ice. Here the challenge was different. Each placement required at least two blows from the ice tools, and the second was effective only if it landed exactly where the first one had already made an inroad. Laborious, yes, but secure and preferable to the uncertainty of the loose snow.

It was steep, steep ice, but above me was a welcome sight: sky, a horizon, the summit ridge! Up I went, conscious and cautious of the real possibility that I was climbing on to a hidden cornice. But no, it was a firm ridge. And there to my right, only metres away, was Jaime at the summit belay. It was 10.15 a.m., four hours since we had left the bergschrund, and we were at 5,947 metres on the summit of Alpamayo, having climbed one of the most spectacular ice faces in the world.

Sadly, there was no panoramic view to match the occasion. The clouds had moved in. A colour printer wasn't necessary for the summit photographs. But being there felt exhilarating. We lingered for nearly half an hour, enjoying every moment, before reminding ourselves that, as ever, the job was only half done.

If Jaime and I were quickish getting up, then we were just plain quick getting down. Top to bottom in an hour and a half. We definitely hit a rhythm on those abseils. However, it did take me a while to get used to the anchors. Nearly all were old 'Vthreads': six- to seven-millimetre rope threaded through holes in the ice that had been carved out with ice screws by previous parties. The anchors of course are only as secure as the ice that holds them in place. Apparently, they are immensely strong – but to the uninitiated, well … a tad unnerving: a bit like abseiling off an icicle.

We recrossed the bergschrund at 12.15 p.m., coiled our ropes, and a quarter of an hour later reached camp. Hugs all round. And reassuring news: Alasdair was fine.

Though the sunset that evening glowed a warming orange, it was at the same time dark and threatening, the dying sun fighting it out with sinister black storm-clouds. The mountain range to the west was silhouetted against the low-angled light, the nearest peaks cast in coal-black shadow, those further from us in progressively lighter shades of grey. It seemed a fittingly dramatic end to a special day.

The next morning, in good order and good spirits, we descended all the way to Base Camp. Fifteen minutes from our tents in the meadow, I stopped, pausing for a moment to take in the greenery, photograph the flowers and – well, chill. Then I resumed my stride and headed for camp and friends and food – and something of a surprise: 'Sangria al Alfredo'. Sometimes, when you think that life is pretty good, it just gets better.

We hiked halfway down the Santa Cruz Valley before mounting horses for the final part of the descent. I am not a rider. It was steep, rocky and slippery, and had terminal – very terminal – drops to the river gorge below. My life was in the hands – well, hooves – of this animal. It seemed to know what it was doing, but its rider certainly did not. One slight slip, one equine error, and my seven-route dream would not make it beyond four. As the horse plunged falteringly down the precipitous, rock-strewn path, I leaned desperately back, partly to stay in balance, partly to avoid the sight of terra firma disappearing beneath me. On each bend, we seemed to get closer to the edge, my body swaying out over an abyss that, contrary to the laws of physics, never seemed to diminish in extent. When I finally dismounted, I could barely stop myself from kissing the ground. Animal and man (but, let's face it, what I cared about was man) had survived. Surely against impossible odds. Surely the most terrifying experience of my life. Although I guess there was that time thirty-four years before, hanging in a crevasse on that other Peruvian mountain not so far away.

Mount Kenya: the Gate of the Mists.

AFRICA

TRAVERSE OF NELION AND
BATIAN, MOUNT KENYA
(KENYA)

East Africa is home to the continent's most impressive mountains, two of which dominate in particular. Mount Kilimanjaro boasts the highest summit at 5,895 metres but, being a comparatively featureless volcano, is a trekking peak and lacks real climbing interest. Mount Kenya, by contrast, is a collection of different peaks – more properly a range or massif – offering a wealth of climbing routes and claiming the continent's second- and third-highest summits. Between these twin summits lays a fabled col, the Gate of the Mists, a region of mixed rock and ice, separating the meteorological northern and southern hemispheres. The natural objective is a full traverse of the massif taking in both summits and col. This, however, is infrequently done, because it requires both full-on summer and full-on winter climbing with all the associated equipment, plus the need, in most cases, for an open bivouac. Popular or not, that was my objective.

Kenya has a special place in my family story. I have enjoyed not just one but two honeymoons there. My natural father having died while I was very young, my mother remarried when I reached eighteen. I gave her away, and my brother was best man. We all went together on the honeymoon to Kenya. This might seem an odd decision for the bridegroom, who had until this point been a bachelor and had no children. But then my stepfather, Jim, was and is a rather special man. My brother and I changed our surnames to his by deed poll a couple of years into the new marriage. The idea of formal adoption, though, never came up, and would anyway have been impossible under English law since we were no longer minors. It was only much later we discovered that Jim, harking as he did from Kentucky, could legally adopt us under US law. And so it came to pass that my stepfather formally became my father at the age of eighty-four, and adopted his two sons of fifty-seven and fifty-eight a full forty years after that honeymoon in Kenya.

My honeymoon with my wife, Rosemary, I refer to as my 'second honeymoon in Kenya', much to her annoyance. This was my first experience of Mount Kenya itself. Over five days we trekked in from the north, via the Teleki Valley; climbed the lowest of the three major peaks, Point Lenana (4,985 metres), which requires some puff but no climbing expertise; and exited to the south-west via Mackinder's Camp. Thus it was that on 3 August 1984 I stood with my new wife on top of my first African summit. It was a wonderful moment. But even then I had a feeling that one day I must return … with a rope.

That 'one day' was very nearly thirty years later, in September 2013. Rosemary, having long ago exchanged the tent for a hotel room and flushing toilet as her preferred holiday accommodation, understandably declined to join me. Instead, I was again in the company of Mark Seaton, the guide with whom I'd climbed so many alpine peaks, including the Eiger. With us we had a local trekking guide, Eddie Mwalimu, and a veritable retinue of cooks and porters in true African style.

Our objective was to traverse the range, taking in both of Mount Kenya's highest peaks, Batian (5,199 metres) and Nelion (5,188 metres). The question was which way to do it: north-to-south or south-to-north? Alpine peaks typically have a sunny southern side and a wintry northern one.

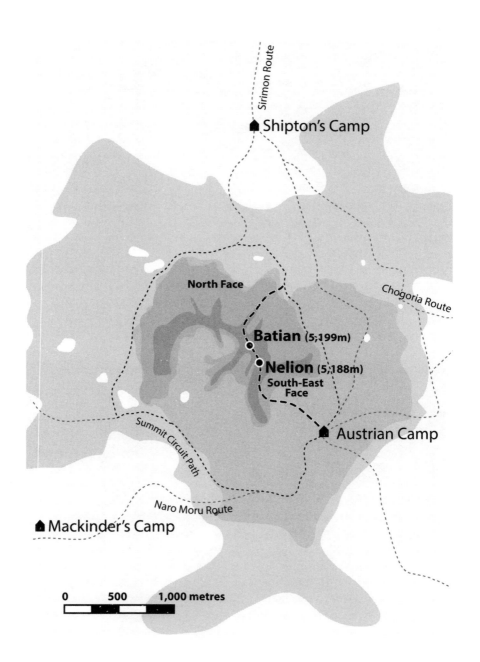

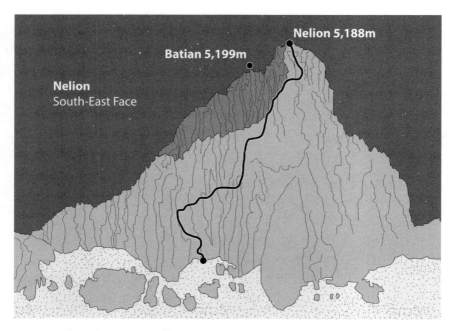

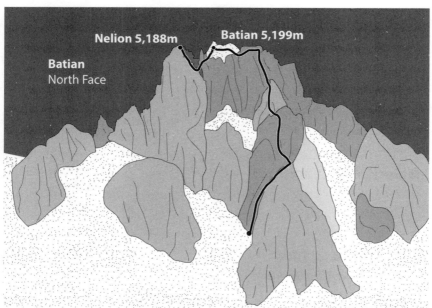

For example, I had climbed the Rébuffat Route on the south side of the Aiguille du Midi with rock shoes and chalk bag, and at a similar time of year the Frendo Spur on the north side with ice axe and crampons. The same is true on Mount Kenya – only with a twist. Because the range is just seventeen kilometres from the Equator, the two sides of the mountain switch seasons during the course of the year. Winter is on the north side during the European winter, and on the south side during the Antipodean winter. On this trip, given it was mid-September, we were there at the tail end of the northern summer, traditionally a good time for climbing on the north side of the range. This suggested that a traverse north-to-south made the best sense. We would aim to climb the north side of Batian, the highest peak, in the warmer, drier conditions; cross the Gate of the Mists to Nelion; and descend the icy rock on the south side with abseils.

We headed north-east out of Nairobi on the Thika road in a Toyota Land Cruiser. There was the usual hurly-burly of a capital city in a developing country, then the inevitable transition through no man's land, where the city gives way to the surrounding country and man's unfinished attempts to tame nature – a rather chaotic jumble of construction: under-planned but underway. Beyond Thika, it became more agricultural, with large pineapple plantations and paddy fields. The *matatu* (minibuses that function as shared taxis) were replaced by motorbikes, donkeys and bullock carts. Everywhere there were vibrant colours, from the red-topped flame trees of Thika fame to the bright-green billboards advertising telecom providers. As the road climbed higher, we entered the zone of coffee, tea, mango and banana plantations. Around midday we pulled off on to a mud road and soon reached Chogoria Lodge, where we parked, somewhat incongruously, next to a large bus of the St Catherine of Siena Girls' High School.

There we transferred to a very old Land Rover. It was a Series II and must have been built more than thirty years earlier, but then the road ahead was not one you would want to subject a new car to: it wasn't so much single track as single tyre. We travelled in convoy with a group of Australians in another, even older-looking, Land Rover. Soon this one had overheated, and we had the bonnet up. It's twenty-six kilometres from the village of Chogoria to the Chogoria Gate on the east side of the Mount Kenya National Park. The Land Rovers managed twenty-one kilometres, but we had to hike the last five kilometres through the bamboo zone, mostly in the rain.

We enjoyed a last night with a roof over our heads in rough cabins at Bandas, just inside the park. Since we were at very nearly 3,000 metres, the process of acclimatisation had already begun. The sun set at 6.30 and rose again at 6.30: on the Equator every day is precisely twelve hours long.

In the morning we hiked for an hour through forests of large trees, hanging epiphytes and a multitude of flowers, including fiery red-hot pokers. The occasional butterfly and electric-blue sunbird fluttered around us. We saw no animals, but there were droppings of elephant, eland and leopard.

We emerged on to rolling, grassy ground and crested Mugi Hill (3,500 metres), our high point of the day, before descending slightly to Lake Ellis, at twenty-eight acres the third-largest of Mount Kenya's great lakes. We pitched a dome-shaped tent for each of us at the water's edge. It had been a fine morning, but soon we were cowering in those tents as rain and then hail lashed down. We were already becoming accustomed to a pattern of clear mornings and heavy afternoon precipitation.

In the mess tent, we enjoyed a dinner prepared by our expedition chef, Lloyd. Initially Eddie and Lloyd chatted between themselves, but soon Mark and I were able to engage them in conversation on those two most ubiquitous of topics: family and football.

Eddie was not a guide whose appearance inspired confidence. He ranked as one of the scruffiest people I had ever met. His black wool hat, faded blue jumper, baggy pants and shapeless jacket all looked as though they had been trampled by a herd of buffalo before the expedition had even begun. By contrast, the Aussies' guide wore a smart ironed shirt and what could have passed for chinos. What became clear over time, though, was that Eddie had no need to advertise his status sartorially. Now in his mid-forties, he had accumulated near-unrivalled experience in supporting trekking and mountaineering groups, and had a level of expertise that everyone respected. In short, he didn't have to try.

As we chatted, the weather cleared and beckoned in a starlit night – again, a pattern that became familiar.

Our route the next day took us on foot over rolling hills, then via a rising ridge up on to cliffs with a deep canyon to our left. We were now entering the so-called Afro–Alpine zone, home to Mount Kenya's two most famous plant families, the lobelias and giant groundsels. These families have countless species, but there seem to be three broad forms overall: one like a giant cabbage; another like a man-sized toilet brush; and a third, larger still, again with cabbage-shaped leaves but this time fixed atop a tall hard stem, like a caricature of a cactus. It seems odd perhaps that such large free-standing plants should grow in this rarefied atmosphere and exposed situation, but nature is a strange mother.

We topped out that day at 4,140 metres before descending sharply and with some difficulty to Lake Michaelson. Mount Kenya's second-largest lake (thirty acres) sits at 3,953 metres and is surrounded on all but its east side by high canyon walls. We camped at the west end, deep in its protective horseshoe, and enjoyed a splendid view out across the water. Despite a clear prohibition, I must admit Mark and I had a skinny dip. This became a rather more public affair than we had planned when the mixed-gender Aussie team descended the path above. I suspect, though, that they were more captivated by the large community of rock hyrax, bounding from boulder to boulder between the tents, than by the puny naked bodies of two pale Englishmen. These curious creatures (that is, the rock hyrax) are similar in size to a marmot or rabbit and yet their closest relatives are apparently elephants and sea cows.

We took our afternoon tea in the company of a large flock of mountain chats, one of which gave Mark an affectionate (or otherwise) peck on the leg, and all of which were after our food. Dinner followed, for us at least if not the chats; and a good night's sleep.

We struck camp just after 9 a.m. and climbed a path beside a series of waterfalls. After a half hour, the route levelled off before resuming ascent more gently up a long, broad valley thronged with the cactus-like giant groundsel and the occasional loo-brush lobelia. There were now real mountain peaks to admire: MacMillan to our left, Delamere ahead and Corydon to our right. But, rather ominously, the three major summits of Mount Kenya itself remained buried in cloud.

The ground steepened again up to a ridge at around 4,600 metres, just beyond which lay a large tear-shaped puddle called Simba Tarn. The cynic in me wondered whether the name was a piece of Disney-inspired branding by the Mount Kenya marketing department, but apparently it related to the sighting of a lion here in 1924. The landscape was more barren than we had experienced thus far, and there were pockets of snow. Meanwhile, in the mess tent, Lloyd served up a welcome lunch of pancakes, tuna and pasta, albeit in that somewhat unconventional order.

We retired for a siesta in the warmth of our sleeping bags just as rain – or was it hail? – began to pound the tents. Later in the afternoon when the pounding stopped, I opened the tent fly – and was shocked. It hadn't been rain or hail. There was a thick carpet of snow on the ground, and more falling. This was supposed to be the dry season! When Mark, Eddie, Lloyd and I, plus all seven porters, huddled in the mess over dinner, the mood was rather flat. Wind buffeted our camp all night long.

We bade farewell to the Aussies in the morning as Mark and I set off with Eddie at 7.30 a.m. Despite the snow underfoot, we quickly reached a shoulder that gave an impressive view down the length of the Sirimon Trail – the one Rosemary and I had used as our approach three decades earlier. We passed the diminutive Harris Tarn and continued on to a summit ridge with a little scrambling, but nothing that required us to give up our trekking poles. There we met a party in descent, the first people we had seen beyond our Aussie friends.

A little further on we found a helpful metal railing which grandly declared itself to be the 'highest via ferrata in the world'. A few tugs and, seventy minutes after leaving our tents, we were on the summit of Point Lenana; at 4,985 metres the high point – in one sense at least! – of my honeymoon with Rosemary. I must admit to a wave of nostalgia.

This was all very well, but it wasn't what we'd actually come to do. We were acclimatising rapidly, but what we now needed was to recce the massif as a whole and figure out how our planned traverse would work. While the porters would transport our gear to Kami Tarn (on the north side) via the short, anti-clockwise route around one-sixth of the range, we would take the much longer clockwise route, allowing a full inspection of the remaining five-sixths.

First, we crossed the so-called Tooth Comb Ridge to reach Austrian Camp (4,790 metres). The huts were eerily deserted but commanded a fine view of our likely descent route down Nelion's icy slabs and across the Lewis Glacier. From there we descended south, and then west on the summit circuit path to reach American Camp (4,350 metres), where we stopped to inspect the legendary Diamond Couloir. This was once Africa's most famous ice climb, but has sadly melted away, a victim of climate change even here at the Equator. A high traverse, a series of pretty tarns and a rather unwelcome flog over Hausberg Col (4,591 metres) eventually delivered us to our tents. These were pitched amongst giant groundsel close to the lower of two very small lakes, known collectively as Kami Tarn (4,425 metres). Since leaving Point Lenana on our circuit of Mount Kenya, we had seen not a single other person. Tent-to-tent it had been a nine-hour day. We were still adjusting to the altitude and both felt tired, so after a splash in the tarn and supper, it was early to bed.

In the morning, Mark and I put on our full climbing gear to investigate the viability of a route up the West Ridge. This would provide a rather enterprising alternative to the North Face of Batian – an approach still from the northern side of the massif, but working along its spine rather than ascending its face. With a lot of scrambling and a certain amount of full-on climbing we reached the ridge at Benuzzi Col (4,830 metres) between Point Dutton to the north and the Petit Gendarme to the south.

Benuzzi Col has an extraordinary story associated with it. In 1943 Felice Benuzzi and two other Italian prisoners-of-war escaped from a British prison camp near Mount Kenya. They knew that escaping from British territory altogether was impossible – they would have had to cover 1,000 kilometres of hostile terrain. Their motivation was a rather different one: bored with the daily routine in the prison camp, they planned a two-week mountaineering holiday to scale Mount Kenya. Guided by a sketch of the mountain taken from a tin of beef, they succeeded in reaching the massif and ascending Point Lenana. Furthermore, two of the men, equipped with ice axes fashioned from hammers, and crampons made of barbed wire, attempted to climb the West Ridge of Batian. It appears that this col is roughly where they got to. A remarkable effort given the circumstances. Having sated their appetites for alpinism, the three then broke back into the prison camp and turned out on parade as normal, much to the astonishment, and it appears grudging admiration, of the British commanding officer. An expected twenty-eight days in solitary was commuted to seven days in recognition of their 'sporting effort'. The whole story is told in Benuzzi's highly entertaining book *No Picnic on Mount Kenya*.

Unfortunately, it was no picnic for us either. We climbed a little above the col to inspect the ridge beyond. Mark was alarmed by the quantity of snow there, especially on the south (winter) side. I suggested giving it a day to see if it would burn off, but I'm not sure even I believed in that prospect. And there was more hail and snow as we made our descent. After much debate back in camp, we decided this was not a viable option.

With the West Ridge approach ruled out, we were now in practical terms committed to a direct attempt on the North Face of Batian. We spent the following day preparing our gear and making a short sortie up to the start of the climbing proper. There we found a plaque to a British couple in their early twenties who had fallen from the North Face in 1990. It turned out that Eddie had been organising their ground support, had had a role in establishing the plaque and had visited the family in the UK. A sad story that somewhat dampened our spirits, as did the heavy thunder and hailstorm that blew in that afternoon.

I cowered in my tent reading H.J. Mackinder's account of *The First Ascent of Mount Kenya*. In 1899 Mackinder, a biologist and geographer from Lincolnshire (who later became the second Director of the London School of Economics and the founder of modern geopolitics), landed in Zanzibar, which had been a centre of the slave trade. At that time, Nairobi was just a station at the end of a railway line that had recently been built from the coast to the interior. It took Mackinder twenty camps and the support of several hundred native tribesmen just to reach Mount Kenya from Nairobi. He entered the massif from the south-west, the route by which Rosemary and I had exited, and reached the summit of Batian on 13 September, little more than a week from our current date. And it appears that he too experienced regular afternoon precipitation.

But, as Eddie assured us, rain was one thing; snow in September was quite another, and almost unheard of. Unfortunately, that was exactly what we were facing. We had a growing feeling that on the north side of the mountain winter had come early. The seasonal window might have closed. Hail and snow kept falling for three and a half hours, and by the time it finished there was no sun left to burn it off. We emerged to an extraordinary but increasingly familiar winter landscape – in equatorial Africa!

Another day was lost. We waited, sitting it out in our respective tents, seething with frustration and breaking the boredom with perfunctory attempts at black humour – 'We should have brought our touring skis.

After all, we are on the Equator.' … and the like. Again it hailed, rained and then snowed. The frustration just mounted further. Our time was all but up. The following day we decided it was now or never.

We reached the foot of the climb at 5.45 a.m. There to our pleasant surprise we found a local guide, David, and his two Swiss clients, Mathias and Aneke. They had come up that morning from Shipton's Camp in the valley below and, like us, planned to attempt the North Face. Though they had arrived first, they were happy to let us set off ahead of them. So, we bade farewell for now to Eddie and our team. And, with my headlamp still lit, I led off up the first technical pitch. The rock was a bit damp in places, but my big boots found adequate edges and there were excellent handholds. I managed easily and quickly. Mark followed through, trending generally right as we switched between moving together and pitching the route (i.e. moving one at a time, always secured by a belay). Shifting back left, we eventually reached a natural amphitheatre of truly Roman proportions. We had made fast progress and it was only 8 a.m.

We exited the amphitheatre at its upper right-hand corner, skirting a huge rock buttress called the Firmin Tower. The gradient and technical difficulty were initially modest, but we did note the increasing presence of verglas. Then suddenly the route seemed to run out. It apparently went up and left, on to the top of the tower – yet it was clogged with ice. Mark was despairing. He called it a full stop. David, now just below us, was in serious conversation with his clients. He announced, 'We should go down.' They were stunned. So was I. One moment we had been romping up; now we were stopped dead and contemplating retreat. David dismissed the idea of going any further and warned us that the Face was unclimbable in these conditions.

Meanwhile, the weather was deteriorating. Cloud was building up, if anything even more quickly than it had in recent days. There would be an afternoon storm, no real question about that. I agonised and procrastinated, desperate to find some route by which we could continue. There wasn't one. An alternative direct assault on the Firmin Tower was out of the question in such conditions and with the storm almost upon us. I wanted to scream with anger – an anger directed at no one other than the weather gods – but screaming wasn't going to help. The climb was over. At least the upwards part of it. We still needed to get down safely. A long series of twenty-five-metre abseils returned us to terra firma around midday. We wished the Swiss team well. Half an hour later we were back at Kami Tarn. As we arrived at the tents, it began to hail, and once again it continued all afternoon. Many days of sunshine would be needed to clear all that ice above, days that were unlikely to dawn before the following season. This one was closed. Our efforts had been for nothing.

We departed the next day down to the valley and Old Moses Camp – a ramshackle collection of buildings reminiscent of a spaghetti western set. Our disappointment about the climb had to be rapidly put aside in the face of a more urgent issue. News from the outside world was now reaching us. Somali terrorists had committed an atrocity at the Westgate shopping mall in central Nairobi, killing at least sixty-seven people and injuring many more. The British Foreign Office was advising against all but essential travel to Nairobi – exactly where we were now headed.

Our remaining energies were devoted to getting home. But this was unfinished business: once again, I had decided that I must return.

Sixteen months later ...

The red crease of dawn spread along the horizon. Mark Seaton, Onex our Tanzanian guide and I watched the opening of a new day on the rooftop of Africa. The snow, the crater, the glacial cliffs and a view of the distant savannah appeared as if from nowhere in the instant that is the lighting of the world on its Equator. We had reached the summit of Kilimanjaro (5,895 metres).

Then others arrived. First Peter, the Belgian we had got to know over the previous five days, and soon everyone else we had passed in recent hours toiling up the scree. They shared a look of collective triumph, their weariness now cast off by the sun and the knowledge that their goal was within grasp. Indeed, within a few minutes, a few steps. They were done, their ascent complete.

By contrast, our journey had just begun. Mark and I felt satisfaction for sure, even elation. But for us, Kilimanjaro was the warm-up, an exercise in acclimatisation for another mountain in another country.

Two days later, Eddie, our now-familiar and trusted Kenyan guide, picked us up at our hotel in Nairobi. As far as I could tell he was wearing the same battered ensemble we had left him in a year and a half earlier. We were delighted to see him.

Again we drove north on the Thika road. There were storks perched on the flat-topped acacia, white egrets pecking on the ground and a black kite wheeling overhead. For the trees, yellow seemed to be the botanical 'in' colour of this particular season. Meanwhile, little boys completed the Merchant-Ivory-like scene, splashing naked in a pond. And everywhere were churches. Lots of churches. Of every denomination I had ever heard of, and a few I hadn't.

There was a distinct sense of déjà vu. Mark and I had been on this road to Mount Kenya before. Defeat had been a bitter blow, but we were determined to try again. This time we were here in January rather than September, so we planned a traverse in the opposite direction, from south to north. Again this would involve crossing hemispheres in meteorological terms from summer into winter, but this time it would be on the southern slabs that we could expect sun-baked summer rock, and on the northern flanks, deep winter snow and ice.

As we drove north, we quizzed Eddie about recent precipitation, and strained to read what we could from the southern aspect of the mountain. Eddie assured us there had been no rain or snow since Christmas Day. This was very good news.

There would be many challenges. One that we would not face, however, was acclimatisation. Mount Kenya is some 700 metres lower than Kilimanjaro, so that issue, at least, we had dealt with.

We pulled over at a town called Karatina, home of one of Kenya's former presidents. A suitable place, we thought, for a lunch to celebrate Mark's fifty-second birthday. We thought wrong. Mark is unlikely to forget his birthday fare of cremated chicken, inedible chips and warm beer! An offer of a return visit later in the trip was politely declined.

Early in the afternoon we passed through the Naro Moru Gate on the south-west side of the Mount Kenya National Park. Nine kilometres further on we found Met Camp (3,000 metres) and pitched our tents for the night. Whereas on Kili we had shared each campsite with at least a hundred other tents, here we shared it with just one. Plus a troop of Sykes' monkeys, who became bolder and more intrusive as time went on: their many misdemeanours included the misappropriation of all our pre-dinner nibbles. Such are the perils of the outdoor life.

Having become accustomed to a higher altitude, Mark and I thought that our lighter sleeping bags would suffice at 3,000 metres. We thought wrong again. It was a bracing night that need not have been.

To recap a little, there are three alternative approaches to Mount Kenya. The northern one, known as the Sirimon Route, was the one I took in 1984 with Rosemary, then my new bride and still wife to this day (somewhat to the surprise of her many sympathisers). The Chogoria Route from the east – without doubt the most beautiful – Mark and I had used in our forlorn attempt of 2013. Now we hiked in from the south-west on the Naro Moru Route, which is short, but often wet underfoot. Indeed, it is famous, or perhaps infamous, for its so-called Vertical Bog.

However, blessed as we were with fine weather, we encountered no such problems. We struck camp at 8 a.m. and strolled in shorts and light fell boots up through the lush montane rainforest, past monkeys and sunbirds and on to the upper meadows dotted with groundsel and lobelia. Once again these giant plants seemed incongruous at such altitude – a bit like coming across a fir tree on the summit of Mont Blanc.

Ahead of us lay Mount Kenya's snow and rock massif, but it looked a long way off. And it felt a long way off as we trekked up the Mackinder Valley, past the camp of like name, and up the steeper path that led to American Camp (4,350 metres) on the mountain's western flanks. We had visited this before, but only in transit. This time it would be our base camp for the trip. We had it to ourselves. Well, us, a murmuration of starlings (the colourful African variety) and a family of rock hyrax, the marmot-like creatures we had met on our last visit.

It was 3 p.m. and we settled in happily to our new surroundings. This was not a hardship assignment. Camping in the mountains has its privations but, as we had discovered before, they are rather less taxing when you have a local guide, deputy guide, chef, waiter and half a dozen guys to carry your kit around, put your tent up, boil your water and generally spoil you rotten. The system is to be recommended. Indeed, I have often wondered whether it couldn't be put to good use in the English Lake District. Sadly, all attempts to persuade my three children to provide such a service have proved in vain.

We were in our sleeping bags with our headlamps off by 8.15 p.m. and slept for ten hours apiece, awaking refreshed to a clear morning. Although we were sufficiently acclimatised to start immediately, we wanted to make a reconnaissance first. Mark and I set off at 8.20 a.m. with Loyford, our deputy guide. For two hours we scrambled up the flank of Point John, past two glacial tarns and – bizarrely – the skeletal carcass of a leopard. At last we skirted the much-diminished Lewis Glacier to reach the foot of Nelion's south-east face at around 4,800 metres. It was a good route for unladen climbers in broad daylight, but not for porters with heavy packs in the dark. Too steep; too exposed. We would need to find an alternative approach. This we did on our return, traversing further east and sliding our way down the tedious, but lower-risk, scree field that forms the glacial moraine.

The next morning, we were away by 3.55 a.m. Eddie and Loyford offered to carry our packs to the foot of the route. We declined, of course … the hell we did! We were delighted to accept, thankful to be able to save our energy for what we knew would be a long day ahead. And so we trudged comfortably at their side as they fought their way up the scree, lit by headlamps and stars.

We reached the rock face proper still in total darkness, but as we stepped into our harnesses and roped up, night turned to day with almost indecent haste. At 6.20 a.m., Mark set off up the steep rock with me in close pursuit. There was no 'Kili crowd', but nor were we entirely alone. Ahead of us was a rope of three: a German guide, Felix, who had studied physics at Nairobi University and knew the mountain well; and his two clients, one also from Germany, the other from the German-speaking Italian Dolomites. They were in big boots; we were in light rock shoes. These were sun-baked slabs and, even early in the morning, better suited to our lightweight, frictional footwear. The difference soon told, and we caught up with them quickly.

The route moved up and left into a gully before traversing back right, exploiting a horizontal weakness. Mackinder's original line up the chimney having fallen out of favour in recent times, we passed it by and climbed the easier One O'Clock Gully to its right. Rapid progress from there, largely moving together, brought us by 8 a.m. to the tin shelter that is Baillie's Bivvy. This small hut – shack might be a better term – has long been abandoned. Its name comes from its constructor, Robert Baillie of the University of Capetown, who opened new routes on Mount Kenya in the early 1960s. Baillie's nickname was Rusty, which, looking at his eponymous bivvy, seemed appropriate. We didn't go inside, but it did make a suitable spot for the five of us to pause, eat and drink, and contemplate the fast-developing morning.

Felix added a layer of clothing and a pair of gloves. Respecting local knowledge, we did the same, and were grateful for the heads-up as we crossed the ridge and descended for a while into the shade. Here we took the lead, bridging our way up a series of chimneys, a foot braced against either wall, to regain the ridge and ultimately the sun. It was excellent rock climbing. An intricate traverse right, flailing around for hidden holds, gave access to a further corner, which took us close to the summit ridge. Some easier scrambling, right again, had us at 10.20 a.m. on the summit of Nelion (5,188 metres), Mount Kenya's second-highest peak. There we found a small bivouac hut and a big view.

The small bivvy was Howell's Hut, and it really was small. Barely a metre from the ground at its highest point and much lower at its entrance, it claimed to accommodate four occupants. Forest pygmies maybe; Maasai warriors definitely not! Its corrugated-iron sections had been deposited on the Lewis Glacier below by helicopter in February 1970 and then carried to the summit of Nelion by a local, Ian Howell, in thirteen separate solo ascents. A remarkable feat. We had no need for it, but the hut is still used regularly to this day, as is evidenced by the countless climbing-club insignias pasted to its exterior.

The big view included our first sight of Batian, our ultimate goal. To reach it we would need first to descend into the col between the two peaks: the celebrated Gate of the Mists with its reputation for ice and swirling fog. Away went the light rubber rock shoes, and out came the big boots and crampons. I went first, down-climbing as far as I could, before the ever-steepening ground forced us into an abseil. Mark joined me at the low point of the col between the two summits. This was a day without the legendary mist, and we stood on benign ground, mainly rock, yet with substantial patches of old snow.

On the other side of the Gate of the Mists, we started upward again, turned a large gendarme (rock tower) and scrambled up easier mixed ground before the route reverted to steep, but firm and reliable, rock on the final exhilarating pitches. These scaled an airy arête, with fine views on either side, before at last arriving at an aiguille-like summit. This was Batian (5,199 metres), Mount Kenya's highest peak and the second-highest point in Africa. Suddenly all the world lay beneath us.

There is nothing very volcano-like about Mount Kenya today, but that's what it was originally. As such, it sits in isolation, which enhances the feeling of height over the surrounding landscape. That day the distant views appeared uninterrupted, and the sense of having arrived somewhere singular and unique was all the more accentuated. Beyond the small expanse of snow that surrounded us lay rocky bastions, then rolling valleys and finally the savannah plain, stretching on all sides to the horizon.

It was 12.50 p.m. The ascent itself had taken six and a half hours and we had been going nine hours from camp. We still felt strong. The other team elected to return via the route they had come up, but we were determined to attempt the full traverse, descending the North Face. This route would involve an initial handful of pitches along the West Ridge. Mark peered down on a vista bespattered with snow and ice. 'This is going to be a long day,' he commented laconically, adding, 'once we go down here, we're committed, because we won't be able to climb back.' Fortunately, I was used to his boundless optimism. He set off and I followed.

The West Ridge was first climbed in ascent in 1930 by a pair of locally based coffee planters described by their biographer, Jim Perrin, as 'the pre-eminent mountain explorers and adventurers of the twentieth century'.[19] These were the soon-to-be legendary Eric Shipton and Bill Tilman, and Perrin rates their first ascent of Kenya's West Ridge as 'probably the finest achievement of pre-war British alpinism'.[20] Amazingly it was also Tilman's first-ever serious climb. Quite a place to start. Shipton and Tilman had also employed the strategy of acclimatising on Kilimanjaro before attempting Mount Kenya. However, somewhat surprisingly given their subsequent achievement, they had not actually made it to the top of Kili. They ascribed this failure to simple exhaustion. In Tilman's own words, 'the reason for our retreat was the ... not uncommon one – inability to go any further.'[21]

The guidebook advertised easy ledges on the left side of the ridge, but that of course was in the summer season. We had now crossed the meteorological hemispheres into winter and a world where every horizontal surface, every ledge, was encrusted with verglas, solid ice or deep snow. We chose instead to keep to the ridge, navigating its crest until we could abseil into a large break called Shipton's Notch.

Here we actually descended too low and had to extract ourselves from an ugly gully before continuing down the West Ridge. We eventually located the line of abseils, off to the right and down the North Face. The first anchor was well equipped with multiple slings and a solid mallion; the next was buried in ice and had to be excavated with an axe; the third was on yet steeper ground and looked distinctly dodgy. We reinforced it, and only when I had checked that it bore Mark's weight did I remove the 'insurance' and descend myself on the original anchor. Thus, we continued with short abseils, often having to hunt for some time to find the anchors, agonising as to whether they were really sound enough. It all felt fairly stressful.

At last we reached a little level ground, but we were still a long way from safety. We knew that there were only a couple of hours of daylight left. Below us lay the Firmin Tower. It was decision time: did we go over the top or round to the left? I favoured the former, because although it would be steeper, I thought the anchors would be easier to find on the rock; Mark favoured the latter, because we already had experience of that ground from our failed attempt at ascent in 2013. We went with Mark's judgement, but were soon questioning that as we found ourselves on ice-covered slabs with not an anchor in sight. We rigged a sling to abseil off. Beyond that we could find nothing secure and had to rely on an old peg that could have dated back to Shipton himself. All the while, the twilight was creeping in. My nerves were starting to get a little ragged.

Mark's nous, though, got us down and we reached the Amphitheatre, where easier ground allowed us to move quickly, unroped. We exited this low down on the left and found a new line of abseils, this time much better equipped. By now it was getting dark. As the ground levelled out a little, we switched on our headlamps and down-climbed the increasingly loose terrain. Soon it steepened again, and I realised that I had never before abseiled in such darkness. Quite a place to learn! But I had plenty of motivation to get it right.

One thing above all had stuck in our minds from our frustrating foray over this ground in 2013: the final abseil lay out of the main gully, far on the right. Now, in the dark, this valuable information came to the fore. Mark found the hidden anchor and first he, then I, descended into the darkness, but in the sure knowledge that firm ground lay below. And there it was, at the very last extremity of the rope, right beside that plaque commemorating the two British climbers killed on this route. A sobering reminder, but we had made it. The descent had taken six and a half hours, the same as the ascent.

Our day was not over. We needed two things for a half-decent night: level(ish) ground we had; water we did not. We knew that Kami Tarn, the campsite we had used on our previous attempt, lay less than 200 metres below us. But where? We stumbled down a boulder field and were soon lost. At one stage I thought I recognised the silhouette of the campsite's one building, a toilet shed, and ran towards it like a desert traveller after an oasis. But it was a giant groundsel, a mirage in the darkness. Exhausted though we were, we had to laugh.

It took a long time to find that tarn, and when we did it was through sheer chance. So much for our night navigation! We had been going eighteen hours and were thirsty, hungry and tired. We collected water, cooked food and brewed tea, lay out our lightweight sleeping bags, put on every stitch of clothing we had, and settled down for a cold, but very happy, night.

This had been a long journey; for me, one starting many decades before. It was now complete. Overhead a shooting star carved a long trace across the night sky. I fancied that, like us, it had started its journey in the southern hemisphere and ended it in the northern one – and like us, had enjoyed at least one brief moment of glory.

Aoraki/Mount Cook: Linda Glacier.

AFRICA

Mount Kilimanjaro: view of Mount Meru from our second camp on Kili.

Middle Dawn at the summit of Kilimanjaro on the roof of Africa.

Bottom Mount Kenya: camping at Michaelson's Lake.

Above The incongruous flora.

Right Mark Seaton bridging the excellent rock on the South-East Face of Nelion, the massif's second-highest peak.

Below The author abseiling into the Gate of the Mists. *Photo: Mark Seaton*

Right The author on the summit of Batian, the massif's highest peak. In the space of a week we had climbed the three highest mountains in Africa. *Photo: Mark Seaton*

Below Mark Seaton descending the upper West Ridge. Once committed, there could be no return.

AUSTRALASIA/
OCEANIA

Wanaka Lake: the perfect base in 'Lord of the Rings' country.

Rippon Vineyard: our base at Wanaka came with all the amenities, including some very fine Pinot Noir.

Slightly less comfortable at the Colin Todd Hut.

Mount Aspiring/Tititea: the author at dawn on the South-West Ridge. *Photo: Eric Ostopkevich*

Left View down the South-West Ridge of Mount Aspiring/ Tititea with the author below. The weather is closing in. *Photo: Eric Ostopkevich*

Above The sculpted summit ridge.

Below The author at the summit of Mount Aspiring/Tititea. *Photo: Eric Ostopkevich*

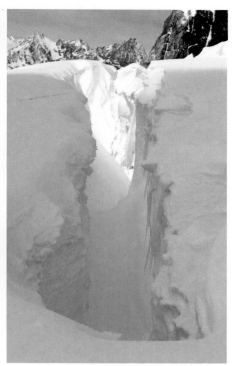

Above Arrival at the Plateau Hut.

Right Crevasse on the Linda Glacier. *Photo: Liza Robi*

Below Dean Staples leading the Zurbriggen Ridge, Aoraki/Mount Cook.

The author on the Zurbriggen Ridge, Aoraki/Mount Cook. *Photo: Dean Staples*

Negotiating the crevasses and weakened snow bridges in descent of Aoraki/Mount Cook.
The author went in to his chest at one point.

ANTARCTICA

Left *Pelagic Australis,* our floating base camp.

Above Falklands to South Georgia:
making sail as we depart Stanley.

Below South Georgia: first landfall, after four days at sea.

Cobblers Cove, probably the safest anchorage on the island.

Stephen Venables approaching Black Peak.

The author, with Stephen Reid, on the true summit of Black Peak.
Photo: Stephen Venables

Stephen Venables on a subsidiary, but perhaps more dramatic, summit.

Grytviken with relics of the past whaling era.

The Whalers' Church. Its library included titles like
Rapture in Rags and *The Reluctant Hussey*.

Locked in the pack ice for four days. Shades of Shackleton. *Photo: Stephen Venables*

Larsen Harbour, arguably the most beautiful anchorage on the island.
Pelagic Australis is just visible.

Top left Male elephant seal staking its claim on the beach at the beginning of the mating season. Harmless unless you happen to be another male elephant seal.

Top middle Fur seal. Not to be messed with. We always kept a sharp ski pole at the ready.

Top right King penguins with *Pelagic Australis* in the background.

Middle Ferrying kit from the shore at Trollhul up on to the plateau.

Bottom left Pinned down for two and a half days and three nights. *Photo: Stephen Venables*

Bottom right Occasionally the weather was bad. Generally, it was worse than that. This became quite serious. *Photo: Stephen Venables*

Above Clear weather at last on the Spenceley Glacier.

Below left Hauling pulks as we thread our way through the crevasse field.
We weren't lost; we just weren't quite sure where we were. *Photo: Kirsty Maguire*

Below right Kirsty Maguire viewing the final descent to St Andrews Bay on the north coast.

The author at St Andrews Bay amidst the world's largest colony of king penguins. *Photo: Stephen Venables*

The expedition team (Skip Novak, Stephen Reid, the author, Stephen Venables and Kirsty Maguire) celebrate on the beach at the end of Day 12. We had taken ten days' food, so we were particularly pleased to be reunited with the others. *Photo: Jennifer Coombs*

Group photo at Government House in Stanley with the Governor, Nigel Phillips CBE, his wife, Emma, and their dog, Gibson. The Governor of the Falkland Islands is also Her Majesty's Commissioner for South Georgia and the South Sandwich Islands. *Photo: unknown*

AUSTRALASIA/ OCEANIA

LINDA GLACIER ROUTE, AORAKI/MOUNT COOK (NEW ZEALAND)

One might have thought that the easiest part of the traditional Seven Summits challenge would be figuring out what the highest peaks on each continent are. Not so in the case of Australasia. This has become a point of contention, with appeals made to everything from simple common sense to advanced plate tectonics. Dick Bass and Frank Wells, the original Seven Summiteers, took the narrow view in the mid-1980s and climbed the highest mountain in Australia: Kosciuszko, at 2,228 metres. With a road to its top (now closed for environmental reasons) and boasting the nation's highest-altitude public toilet, this hillock is not exactly the stuff that great mountaineering challenges are made of.

The Bass and Wells view was subsequently called into question by no less an authority than Reinhold Messner, arguably the greatest climber who has ever lived. Messner drew a distinction between the country of Australia and the continent of Australasia (or, as some prefer, Oceania). The highest point on the latter is the much more demanding, and at 4,884 metres twice as high, Carstensz Pyramid (Puncak Jaya) in Indonesia.

Neither Australia nor Indonesia has a rich history of mountaineering, but they share their continent with a country that certainly does:

New Zealand. Kiwi guides and climbers, emanating largely from the South Island town of Wanaka, have reached around the globe. And let us proud Brits not forget that the summit pair on the 'British' expedition that first conquered Everest in 1953 were a Nepalese and a New Zealander. Indeed, it's said that more Everest ascents have been made by residents of Wanaka and its neighbouring villages than by those of any similar region outside the Khumbu. It was clear to me that my sixth climb should be in New Zealand – although I will admit to some surprise when I got there …

New Zealand may be the cradle of southern-hemisphere climbing, but at first sight its mountains seem rather tame. Their very name, the Southern Alps, conjures an image of a softer, less hazardous version of their 'proper' northern cousins. Even their highest and most formidable massif, Aoraki/Mount Cook, reaches only 3,754 metres, a full kilometre below the summit of Mont Blanc.

As I strolled in the sunshine through Wanaka, that feeling of confident assuredness was only reinforced. New Zealand's most famous mountain range lines the west coast of its South Island. Since the prevailing weather is from the west, it acts as something of a barrier. The remainder of the island enjoys a deceptive calm, characterised by blue skies, verdant valleys, glistening lakes and rolling vineyards.

Nor does Wanaka itself dispel in any way this sense of tranquillity. Large enough perhaps to be designated a small town, it nonetheless feels very much like a village. There is none of the frenetic madness of Chamonix. Instead of nightclubs, Irish pubs and burger chains, there are bohemian bars and relaxed coffee shops, many of them looking out over the clear blue lake with its semi-submerged tree and grassy islands to the snow-capped mountains beyond.

A short walk along the lakefront brought me to Rippon vineyard, whose grapes grow down to the water's edge. I popped in for a wine tasting – not the standard preparation for a mountaineering expedition, but one has to build up the calorific reserves somehow. The Pinot Noir is to be particularly recommended. Later I discovered that the local cinema, with its single screen and cosy auditorium, still observed the tradition of an interval, during which warm homemade brownies were served: yet further calorific reinforcement.

The locals are as warm and welcoming as their cookies. I spent a couple of very pleasant evenings with Nick Cradock and his family. Nick pioneered many of the nearby rock and ice routes before settling into a career as a climbing and heli-skiing guide. I had skied with him twice in the past: on the edge of the Arctic Circle in Eastern Greenland, and more recently high in the Indian Himalaya. Now we sat under a clear blue sky at the edge of Wanaka Lake, drinking locally brewed craft beer and enjoying a late supper, warm enough wearing just thin pullovers, even long after the sun had set. It was hard to imagine that this was the rugged base from which the country's deeds of alpine derring-do were planned and prosecuted. So it was to come as a bit of a jolt when I was rudely awakened to the kind of challenge these mountains and their weather fronts could offer.

But, before that could happen, I needed to resolve a question that is crucial to any mountaineering expedition: which mountain to climb? My previous trips had involved some calm research/reconnaissance and much less calm debate as to what constituted each particular continent's finest climb. But, in all cases, that choice was made before reaching my selected destination. New Zealand was a little different. I arrived there with two possible objectives, unsure which really had claim to the top spot. The range of high mountains on the South Island's west coast is really two ranges, one dominated by Mount Aspiring (or Tititea in the indigenous language), the other by Mount Cook (Aoraki, to give it its local name). The former's south-west ridge is rated by many as the classic ice climb in the country; the latter's Linda Glacier Route as the classic mixed climb. Torn by indecision, I thought 'Why not try both and then decide?'

For the attempt on Mount Aspiring/Tititea, I teamed up with a Canadian guide from the Bugaboos, Eric Ostopkevich of Adventure Consultants. In the winter, Eric was a heli-skiing guide in British Columbia, but he was now getting some climbing done at the opposite end of the world before that season got underway. A positive, affable young man in his thirties, with a tireless concern for those around him, he was impossible not to like. I took to him instantly. And my enthusiasm for Eric only increased when I tasted his cooking. We headed into the hills with a generous supply of fresh food and he proved an excellent chef. There was to be no rehydrated chilli con carne on this trip.

The summits of the Southern Alps may be lower than those in Europe, but somehow the mountains *feel* bigger. The terrain is vast. And with the favourable weather windows so short, this pretty much necessitates the use of helicopters on the approach. If you walk in during fine weather, you will almost certainly be doing the proper climbing in a storm.

Our heli picked us up at Raspberry Creek, an hour's drive outside Wanaka. A fifteen-minute flight delivered us from luxuriant green meadows to a snow-bound Bevan Col (1,851 metres), poised above the Bonar Glacier. We strapped on our crampons and descended 150 metres to the glacier, our eyes fixed ahead on the looming mass of Mount Aspiring/Tititea (3,033 metres). The mountain was given its modern name in 1857 by the surveyor J.T. Thomson, who described his awe at this 'glorious pyramid of ice and snow'.[22] To me, this almost symmetrical triangle, piercing the heavens above, seemed like a child's conception of a mountain. As I viewed it, my eyes were drawn to the mountain's right flank. There a majestic white arête rose from right to left, against a deep blue skyline, reaching all the way to the summit, broken in just one place by an overhanging rock band. This was the south-west ridge, our objective for the morrow.

Our immediate task, though, was to reach a hut, specifically the Colin Todd Hut (1,799 metres), a bright red metal construction which we could see perched on a rock above us, looking rather like a fire engine that had taken a seriously wrong turning. We arrived there to be greeted by the only others currently in residence: a flock of parrots. This was not the scene I had expected. These were, as Eric explained, kea: an alpine parrot that is endemic to the South Island. Quite large for a parrot, they had green-brown plumage, yellow-ringed eyes and a long curved beak capable of killing a sheep. This last habit had got them into trouble with the local farming community and sadly left them endangered. The hut was clearly a sanctuary and, no doubt, an occasional source of food.

For the moment, we had at least the interior of the building to ourselves. This comprised a small vestibule for outdoor gear and a single living room with sixteen bunks on two tiers, a long dining table and an extensive cooking area. It was now late afternoon and other parties started to arrive. It wasn't long before the hut was at full capacity.

There was a regular radio call at 7 p.m. to get a detailed weather forecast. It was not good: a front was rolling in and would bring strong winds and heavy precipitation. All the other groups decided they would retreat to the valley first thing in the morning. Eric, to his great credit, was not prepared to give up entirely, but he did understandably pare back our objective from the more ambitious south-west ridge to the less demanding and less committing ordinary route up the so-called Ramp.

Sure enough, come the morning we were the only ones headed up rather than down. Having arisen at 2 a.m., we were away shortly thereafter. Roped up, with an axe in one hand, a ski pole in the other, we worked our way along a clear-enough track in the snow, skirting the mountain's north-west ridge. Our path was lit by our headlamps and a panoply of stars. I couldn't help but notice that the constellation of Orion was the wrong way up – or, at least, the wrong way up if you came from the planet's other hemisphere. It was all a bit like driving on the other side of the road.

We made rapid progress. Meanwhile, the usually convivial Eric went quiet on me. He was clearly deep in thought. He stopped, paused and then turned to face me. He had never climbed the south-west ridge. Would I mind if we gave that a try after all? I was delighted.

We reached the foot of the Ramp and there the track ran out. It appeared that everybody before us, at least those who had come this way since the last snowfall, had taken the regular route, turning up the mountain at this point. From here we would be breaking our own trail.

We continued to traverse the slope, albeit zigzagging a little to gain height. As the gradient increased, we exchanged our ski poles for a second ice tool each and Eric drove in the occasional picket for protection. These pickets are essentially large metal stakes, hammered into the snow slope, with a karabiner attached, through which the rope is fed. They are rarely seen in Europe but seem well-suited to the heavily snow-laden slopes typical of the Southern Alps.

We reached the south-west ridge just as dawn broke in a cacophony of orange. It was a beautiful, but also a sobering, sight. Beneath the rising sun lay a deep charcoal-black carpet of storm-clouds – for sure, the much-heralded big front. The cloud was already rising from the valley and invading the lower ramparts of our far-from-impregnable bastion. There was no time to lose. We turned to the ridge above us. You could have marked the route with a pencil, so well-defined was the knife-edge crescent that rose in a gracious curve, highlighted by the contrast of the dawn sun on its right side and the remaining shadow of night on its left.

We climbed as quickly as we dared, until forced to pause and assess the remaining rock barrier that stood between us and the final summit slopes. Here steep, rather featureless slabs forced us into a couloir on the left, where a two-metre-wide ribbon of sixty-degree ice offered the only feasible route of ascent. We hacked out a platform at its foot, where I could establish a firm belay. Eric led off, while I paid out the rope. He worked his way up on the front points of his crampons, each placement of his twin ice tools requiring two, or even three, strikes to achieve a reliable hold. To protect himself, he inserted a cam and then an ice screw, but after that he could find neither cracks in the rock nor thick enough ice for further gear. It became a case of 'you must not fall'. Fortunately, the most challenging ground was sustained for just a single pitch (roughly sixty metres). I followed and soon we regained the ridge proper. Now we could see the summit itself, standing proud aloft a final sculpted ice arête. It was a dramatic landscape with severe drops especially on the south side, but the way was carpeted in perfect *névé* and we ascended easily enough, topping out at 8.30 a.m.

Like so many mountains, Mount Aspiring/Tititea's history has a certain pathos to it. The first person to stand on this summit in 1909 was Major Bernard Head of the Royal Welsh Fusiliers. Six years later he was to fall to a sniper's bullet while attempting to scale the cliffs at Gallipoli.

The cloud had now risen on every side, obscuring completely all the nearby peaks. It was as if we were on a lone island surrounded by a foaming sea. The only other summit still visible was that of Aoraki/Mount Cook far off to the north. We took a half-hour break to eat and drink but dared not stay longer.

The initial descent down the north-west ridge was straightforward. The gradient was undemanding and the visibility good. But, as we dropped down into the cloud, we lost all points of reference. The terrain steepened. Then it started to snow. And that snow was soon coming at us horizontally, driven by strong wind. Moving together in such conditions was just too risky, so it was slow work as we climbed one at a time down nine pitches. Momentarily disoriented, I lost my way and got too far right, soon finding myself on a perilously thin veneer of ice over rock. I tried to traverse back left, lost my footing and took quite a swinging fall, eventually arrested as the rope at last came back into the vertical.

There remained one further technical challenge: getting down the Ramp. The Ramp itself proved relatively benign, as the name might have suggested, but it was broken by a large crevasse, a bergschrund, blocking the route. Eric lowered me to its upper lip, where I clipped the rope into a snow picket. Then I gingerly climbed down into the fissure and equally cautiously up the other side, before belaying Eric as he did the same. In the deteriorating conditions this proved quite a nerve-wracking finale, but by 12.30 p.m. we were back in the safety of the Colin Todd Hut.

We had been out nine and a half hours, a comparatively short time. This was no bad thing, because now the storm struck with its full force. We were alone in the hut and pinned down by a ferocious wind and driving snow. The whole fabric of the hut shook. Even the outside toilet was too risky a venture. Instead, a metal bucket had to be pressed into service.

The next day the weather abated somewhat, allowing a four-hour excursion to traverse the aptly-named Rolling Pin (2,251 metres), a narrow, mostly snow-covered, ridge with impressive views (and drops) to either side. Again, we returned to a hut empty but for us. It snowed again that night ... and all the following day ... and the following night.

We awoke for the fourth time in the Colin Todd Hut, determined to escape. I managed to reach Rosemary on the satellite phone. It was a good thing I did, because she and my family were distraught. The storm had downed a helicopter on the Fox Glacier on Aoraki/Mount Cook, killing seven people, including four Britons. They had feared I was among them. My call at last relieved their anxiety.

Fairly obviously, getting out by helicopter was not on the cards. We would need to walk out, which would take two days, assuming it was possible at all. The weather had improved for the moment, but with twenty-five centimetres of fresh snow, the avalanche hazard was high. We descended to the Bonar Glacier (1,600 metres). No sooner had we reached this featureless white expanse than once more the mist moved in, leaving us unable to navigate other than by compass and GPS. Still, we continued, climbing up to a flat plateau, the so-called Quarterdeck, and on to its eponymous col (2,290 metres), positioned beneath the reassuringly named Mount Avalanche.

We knew that on the other side lay treacherous terrain with the dramatic cliffs of the equally heartening Gloomy Gorge. Fortunately, our luck turned and at this moment the mist cleared. Eric led, cutting steps down the ice to reach the much easier glacier below and, before long, the French Ridge Hut (1,483 metres). This was a spacious hut, twice the size of the Colin Todd. Once more we had it to ourselves. It seemed that we were the only ones out in these hills. But at least we were now on safe ground. The next day a 1,000-metre descent over eighteen kilometres of largely forested country – completed almost entirely in torrential rain – returned us to Raspberry Creek and our car.

It had been a challenging excursion and a little recovery time was needed. A traverse of the Remarkables (2,319 metres), a rock ridge dominating the skyline over Queenstown, and a couple of days of valley rock climbing fitted the bill rather well. Plus, of course, more wine and warm cookies.

I was now ready to tackle my other objective: Aoraki/Mount Cook, New Zealand's highest peak. The mountain's very name emphasises its importance. In 1998 the Crown agreed that, for various features of the South Island, Maori place names should be included alongside the existing Europeanised ones. In all cases the Maori name was placed after the Europeanised one. In all cases, that is, bar one: for Mount Cook, the Maori name, Aoraki, would come first. Such was the significance to the indigenous people of this highest peak. As one of the first ascensionists put it, using a still older name for the mountain, 'there is but one Aorangi.'[23]

For this project I turned to something of a New Zealand legend, Dean Staples. One of the country's most renowned guides, Dean is a veteran of more than twenty expeditions to over 6,000 metres, including nine Everest ascents. He is quietly spoken, indeed taciturn to the point of introversion, his vast experience and unquestionable competence finding expression through deed not word. He has a calm determination, and is neither easily excited nor easily deflected – the kind of person you can rely on to see things through, as I was soon to discover.

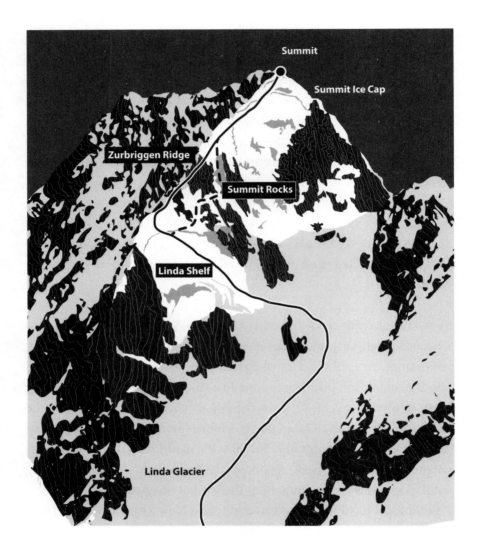

The drive to Aoraki/Mount Cook Village took three hours, and we arrived in pouring rain. We visited the alpine museum, which includes a prominent photograph of Dean's partner, Lydia Bradey, whom I had last seen high on Ama Dablam. Dinner followed and a restful night at a lodge run by the New Zealand Alpine Club.

Our heli took to the sky – a now clearing sky – at 9.40 a.m. and gave us a brief scenic tour of Aoraki/Mount Cook and its spectacular Grand Plateau before depositing us and our gear at the Plateau Hut (2,200 metres). This is a substantial refuge with bunks for thirty-three, many of which were already occupied when we arrived. A walkabout on the neighbouring ridges to acclimatise and to rehearse skills one last time, lunch, rest and dinner filled the remainder of the day.

It was an early-morning start, or strictly speaking a late-evening one: we rose from our bunks at 11.45 p.m. A little over an hour later, we were away, the first to leave the hut. Close on our heels were a further two guide-and-client pairs. An American team stayed behind, having decided they weren't ready for an attempt that day.

Our route was the classic one up the Linda Glacier. We started by descending to around 2,100 metres before climbing up through the crevasse field. There had been a heavy snowfall, but fortunately another pair had decided to get a head start by bivouacking further up, and they had put in a track. With big 'holes' on either side, care was needed, and we had our axes ever at the ready. But in the main it was a relaxed climb with just poles and crampons – lit by our headlamps. We continued in this fashion for three hours, stopping only to bury a cache of water in the snow, noting carefully the terrain so that we could retrieve it later.

Then our luck rather ran out. On the shoulder left and above us we could see the lights of the pair still at their bivouac. We knew them to be a young Italian guide, nicknamed 'Fast Freddie', and his client Liza, an experienced South Island climber. Unfortunately, they would now be coming up behind us, which of course meant no more track. The going immediately became much tougher. Dean, at the front, was sinking with each step up to his knees and sometimes beyond. Soon he was tiring. This was hardly surprising. Both in our fifties, neither of us was quite as spring chickenny as we once might have been. It was clear that we would need to share the task of breaking trail. I offered to lead for a while and Dean sensibly accepted.

129

Higher up, the route steepened. I seemed to be up to my waist in snow and any progress came at a huge cost in physical effort, but happily this was short-lived. We reached a bergschrund and Dean resumed the lead, confidently straddling the void. With two tools, he hauled himself over and traversed up and left across the Linda Shelf. We had now gone from too much snow to too little: from waist-high drifts to rock-hard ice. At the top of this shelf lay another, larger and more problematic bergschrund, which ultimately yielded to front points and swings of axe and hammer. It gave access to a wide gully that felt a little easier. Dean got a 'stopper' (metal wedge) in the rocks on the left and a sling over a pinnacle, protecting our progress as we ascended. At the top we moved left and joined the Zurbriggen Ridge, named after the Swiss guide Matthias Zurbriggen, who via this route made the second ascent of the mountain in March 1895. In one sense, Zurbriggen might also be credited with the first ascent. It's said that it was his imminent arrival in New Zealand in late 1894 that spurred the locals to renew their efforts on the country's highest peak before it was snatched by a foreigner.

Having at last reached the beginning of the real Summit Rocks, we were no longer alone. Our slow progress breaking trail lower down had allowed Fast Freddie and Liza to catch up. But the steepening slope, bullet-hard ice and resulting need for sustained front-pointing had taken its toll on the others. One of the clients had been on his fourth attempt at the mountain. The other already had six of the seven summits under his belt and had never before failed on a peak. Both had turned for home. From here on, it would be just the four of us.

Ahead lay near-vertical rock plastered with wind-blown ice. The ice was too thin to take the point of an axe or crampon, and too slippery to offer any other kind of purchase. It was beginning to look like a scenario from a disaster movie. It occurred to me that Dean might want to call the climb. But although the conditions underfoot (and hand) were pretty extreme, the weather overhead remained fine. Dean merely commented that we would be pitching it – climbing one at a time – all the way from here to the top, and I had better be prepared for a long day.

This was now classic mixed climbing: rock and ice. Since the lead climbers would inevitably be sending down a quantity of debris on to the heads of those below, the two pairs tacitly agreed to take different lines. Freddie and Liza took the arête on the left, while Dean and I climbed the face slightly further right. Even so, various consignments of ice and rock came careening my way, one of which knocked out my headlamp. There was something strangely familiar about that. But thankfully, its task was complete for the day.

Four steep pitches, protected by slings, ice screws and pickets, brought us eventually to a shallow shoulder. Even here, though, we had to take great care. The gradient was undemanding, but the ice still refused to yield. Front-pointing with two tools on such a modest slope was backbreaking work – like climbing a gentle hill while bent over on all fours.

After two or three further pitches, we tried moving together, traversing up and right. It was nerve-wracking, because it was clear that neither of us would be able to hold the other if he fell. We were tiring but took heart from the sight of the younger pair topping out. We dug a bit deeper, resumed pitching, once more heading straight up, and in two and a half rope spans were at last on the summit. It was midday.

Strictly speaking we were a metre or so below the summit (3,754 metres). Aoraki/Mount Cook is sacred to the indigenous people. In their mythology, Aoraki is one of the sons of Ranginui, the Sky Father. There is an understanding that climbers do not stand on the summit itself. We respected this, of course. Nonetheless, we enjoyed a panoramic view back to the east, down the ridge and over the snow-laden glacier we had just climbed; and for the first time now to the west, where the vista continued down to the coast and Tasman Sea beyond.

The mountain was first climbed on Christmas Day 1894 by a team of New Zealanders keen, as we saw, that this crucial peak should be bagged first by the home team. Such was their excitement that, so it is reported, they ran up the final section to the summit. Clearly, they experienced conditions rather different from ours! Dean commented that he had climbed Aoraki/Mount Cook probably twenty-five times, but never seen the ice so hard. Freddie made a similar observation later in the hut – 'sketchy' was the word he used. We felt very satisfied to have made the ascent, but descending the ice looked daunting, and we had no doubt it would draw on all our reserves.

We spent a half hour on the top, cramming down our throats as many calories as possible, before Dean lowered me off and followed, down-climbing. The sun was at last softening the ice, allowing our tools to be used in dagger fashion rather than being swung exhaustingly overhead. We abseiled the summit blocks. It was slow work, because many of the anchors required digging out, inspecting properly and then reinforcing. Care was needed recrossing the bergschrund, and speed as we traversed the exposed Linda Shelf. We were now directly below the so-called Gun Barrels, which were living up to their name as sun-loosened ice and rock rifled down on all sides. We moved as rapidly as we dared, but even so took more than one direct hit. This was particularly concerning because any fall could all too easily have ended in a crevasse, many of which gaped below.

We were grateful to reach our cache of water at 6 p.m. and took a half-hour break. The threat from above was now replaced with a threat from below. I led our way back through the minefield of crevasses, across now-sun-weakened snow bridges. I sank waist-deep into one of them. Fortunately, I was on my guard, reacted promptly yet calmly, lay flat to distribute my weight, and sort of 'swam' out. It wasn't elegant; however, it worked. Much emphasis is put on crevasse rescue, but in truth self-extraction is your best bet. The final 100-metre climb back up to the hut was not entirely welcome. With the end in sight, though, our spirits rose to the occasion.

We reached the Plateau Hut (2,200 metres) at 8.15 p.m. We had been going nineteen hours and twenty-three minutes with only the briefest of respites. It had not been my hardest day of climbing, but it had certainly been my longest. The climb on Mount Aspiring/Tititea had been challenging for sure, but this had pushed me to a further degree. The length of the route, the unrelenting ice, the extended threat from both rockfall and crevasse – but also the beauty and wildness of the surroundings, the significance of this massif to the local people, and that view down to the distant ocean – all these had reinforced my respect for New Zealand's premier mountain, Aoraki/Mount Cook. I felt I had found, to my satisfaction at least, the continent's finest route.

I slept well in the hut that night. Nick Cradock was there too and up at 4 a.m. for a training exercise with his clients. Before he left, he brought me a cup of tea in my bunk. A very civilised, very typical Kiwi gesture.

The next evening, back in Wanaka at the Cinema Paradiso, I watched *The Program*, the film about the world-leading cyclist Lance Armstrong and his dramatic fall from grace. It reminded me of a motivational talk given to my firm by Sean Fitzpatrick, the ex-captain of the New Zealand All Blacks. The thrust of his message had been that winning, and only winning, was what really mattered. I am not suggesting for a moment that Sean Fitzpatrick ever cheated or even considered cheating. After all, his achievements as a sportsman, media commentator and philanthropist are extraordinary. But I fundamentally disagree with him on this point. There is so much more to life than winning. And this is true of climbing too: there is so much more than just getting to the top. Indeed, getting to the top in itself is really rather meaningless. Or, to express it differently, getting to the top draws its true satisfaction not in isolation, but from its association with so many other things: the people you climb with, the history of those who went before, the expected and unexpected challenges that must be overcome, the aesthetic nature of the terrain and the special character of the country you explore in the process. My two and a half weeks in New Zealand had certainly delivered on all those things.

The author on the Spenceley Glacier. *Photo: Stephen Reid*

ANTARCTICA

COAST-TO-COAST TRAVERSE OF THE
SALVESEN RANGE, SOUTH GEORGIA
(UK OVERSEAS TERRITORY)

I was enjoying my Full English Breakfast (£8.95 all-in) in the West Café, which commanded an enviable view over the seafront of this well-kept, rather pretty and gaily coloured seaside town. Outside, the water was calm, lapping up to the coastal road, which boasted a traditional red phone kiosk and matching pillar box. It could have been one of any number of British seaside towns … but it wasn't. Three things indicated otherwise: first, the huge number of Union Jacks flying everywhere – too many, as though someone were seeking to make a point, which indeed they were. Second, the presence of a red London double-decker bus, looking strangely out of place by the sea; and third, the name of the local newspaper open in front of me: the *Penguin News*. I was in fact 8,000 miles from the likes of Salcombe, Frinton and Torquay. I was in Port Stanley in the Falkland Islands.

You will have surmised by now that these seven climbs have been largely an excuse to travel the world, visiting all manner of fascinating places. This was never truer than of the last of the seven. But the planning for this seventh expedition had its roots in the aftermath of the first climb – and firmly in London.

I was attending an evening of lectures on the North Face of the Eiger, held at the Royal Geographical Society in Kensington. At the end, all those present who had climbed the Face were invited to come up on stage. Having arrived straight from work and feeling rather self-conscious in my business suit, I slipped a little deeper into my seat and pretended not to hear. To no avail. The friends I was with pushed me up on to the platform, where I felt uncomfortably out of place among such luminaries as Sir Chris Bonington, Ueli Steck and Stephen Venables. Sir Chris had of course put up the first British ascent of the Eigerwand, while Ueli Steck held the speed record (sadly, Ueli later died climbing solo on Nuptse in the Himalaya). For Stephen Venables, the Eigerwand was more of a rite of passage, a precursor to his remarkable ascent of Everest without supplemental oxygen and via a new route, the Kangshung Face.

I was a bit star-struck, but not to such an extent that I couldn't eagerly exchange contact details with Stephen when he asked. In the nicest possible way, he was clearly thinking 'Who the hell is this guy and what's he doing up here?' Anyway, one thing led to another, and before I knew it Stephen was asking me to join an expedition to South Georgia in the South Atlantic.

I wasn't actually sure where South Georgia was. I had a vague recollection that the Argentines had invaded it days before landing in the Falklands, thus igniting the 1982 conflict. But where exactly was it and to which continent did it belong? Crucially, could it reasonably be classified as Antarctic, and thus possibly furnish my seventh route? Soon I was grappling with a piece of trivia that proved much more complicated than it might at first sound: what is Antarctica?

Faced with this question, I was initially tempted to consult my wife, Rosemary, who after all took a First at Cambridge in Geography and Education. But then I remembered she had always thought Bogotá was a country in Africa. So, I turned instead to the textbooks.

Definitions of Antarctica abound. The narrowest of the popular delineations would be 'everything within the Antarctic Circle'. That is, the area of our planet south of the 66th Parallel, which experiences at least one day of continuous daylight every year (the December solstice) and a corresponding period of continuous night-time (the June solstice). This is deeply problematic, though, because it excludes a significant part of the main Antarctic land mass and, notably, the whole northern section of the Antarctic Peninsula.

That leaves two alternative competing definitions: the political one and the scientific one. The dominant political definition is everything south of the 60th Parallel. This is the area stipulated in Article VI of the 1959 Antarctic Treaty, which suspends all national (that is, 'colonial') claims to territorial rights in the region. Such claims are maintained by Chile, Argentina, the UK, Norway, France, Australia and New Zealand – and importantly are only suspended, not cancelled. It also prohibits exploitation of natural resources. Only scientific research, exploration, fishing and non-invasive tourism are permitted. This definition has the virtue of encompassing the whole of the main Antarctic land mass. However, it is a highly arbitrary cut-off, unlike any boundary used to define any other continent. And it doesn't even attempt to reflect the 'contours of nature'. This political designation of Antarctica excludes South Georgia (it lies roughly between the 54th and 55th Parallels), which is why the island is able to remain under solely British administration.

The leading scientific definition of Antarctica follows the contour of the Southern Ocean, known as the Antarctic Convergence (or, some-times, the Antarctic Polar Front), where the cold waters of the Southern Ocean meet the warmer waters of the more northerly equatorial seas. It is this boundary that reflects most closely the unique natural character-istics of Antarctica: the physical appearance of the terrain; the climatic conditions, including precipitation levels; and the krill population that supports the region's fish, birds and mammals. Although the Antarctic Convergence does shift from year to year by up to fifty kilometres, South Georgia always falls well within its domain. This explains why the island is such a vast breeding ground for everything from albatrosses to penguins to fur, elephant, leopard and Weddell seals; and why its surrounding waters host such large numbers of dolphins and whales (when not hunted to near extinction). Thus, from a naturalist's perspective, South Georgia is very much a part of Antarctica.

The more I learnt about South Georgia, the more the island seemed to reflect the essential characteristics of the continent that I was keen to capture. Despite extensive exploration, Antarctica remains largely a wilderness. It is the only continent with no indigenous (human) population, and it still receives very few visitors considering its vast size. And those visits are mostly concentrated in the handful of areas that are comparatively accessible. These include the area around Union Airport, which services many of the more adventurous activities, including ascents of Mount Vinson, one of the Seven Summits; the Ross Ice Shelf, which is visited regularly by cruise ships from New Zealand and Tasmanian ports; the bases at the South Pole; and, above all, the Antarctic Peninsula, which is ice-free in summer and easily (well, comparatively easily) accessed from South America. By contrast, South Georgia remains without an airport and is sufficiently remote by sea to deter most casual visitors. Furthermore, Stephen proposed we travel to the interior of this 100-mile-long island in the early spring, where and when we could reasonably hope to be the only humans.

The other essential character of the Antarctic that I sought to experience was that of the journey. If you think of the great figures of Antarctic exploration, they have generally not been mountaineers, but rather those bound on a journey: Cook, Weddell, Ross, de Gerlache, Drygalski, Charcot, Amundsen, Scott, Filchner, Mawson and Shackleton – men (and they were all men) focused less on the vertical than the horizontal. They aimed to get somewhere *over* there rather than somewhere *up* here. What attracted me about the South Georgia itinerary was that same sense of journey: sailing from the Falkland Islands to South Georgia, skinning on skis into the southern Salvesen Range, and hopefully dragging our pulks (sledges) over a series of high cols to complete a crossing from coast to coast. To my way of thinking, that was truly Antarctic.

Added to that, of course, was South Georgia's unique historic legacy associated with Sir Ernest Shackleton's sea voyage, and his traverse of the island in a bid to reach help for his stranded men. It is an extraordinary story. On 8 August 1914, as war broke out across Europe, Shackleton's hand-picked team set off from Plymouth in *Endurance*, their objective to achieve the first traverse of the Antarctic continent. Their last port of call was Grytviken on South Georgia. From there they motor-sailed into the Weddell Sea, searching for a suitable place to land the shore team. Before they could do so, *Endurance* became trapped and then crushed in the pack ice, leaving Shackleton and his men to drift north on the ice floes until they could make a landing in small boats on Elephant Island. Since there was little hope of their ever being found there, Shackleton and five others took to the sea again in the twenty-two-and-a-half-foot cutter *James Caird* in a desperate attempt to find help on South Georgia. The 800-mile trip took them three weeks and, when at last they got there, they still had to land and undertake the first-ever traverse of the island. They succeeded, eventually raising help from the whaling station at Stromness. After many abortive attempts and with much assistance from the Chilean government among others, Shackleton was able to relieve his men on Elephant Island on 30 August 1916 – some two years after departing Britain.

Remarkably, not one of those on *Endurance* lost his life. And it might even be argued that this gruelling journey into the Southern Ocean actually saved many of them. These men, after all, were of fighting age and in many cases already serving soldiers or seamen. The alternative would have been the trenches of Flanders and/or the beaches of Gallipoli with all the perils that entailed.

For these various reasons – the sense of a wilderness to be explored, the desire to make a journey in keeping with the continent's tradition and the enthralling history tied to that – I felt South Georgia was the ideal place to go looking for my seventh route.

There was one further attraction: our planned route would be completed almost entirely on skis. British climbers have traditionally seen mountaineering and skiing as distinct pursuits. By contrast, continental European climbers have long acknowledged a continuity between the two. The line between ski touring and ski mountaineering is at best a blurred one. Many of my biggest alpine ascents had been on skis and I was keen that this should be reflected somewhere in my seven climbs.

Back at the West Café, I finished my breakfast and went for a stroll along the front in rare sunshine to take in the charms of Stanley. On this quiet Sunday morning there were few others around, but I did pass an Argentine family. They smiled in greeting and I wished them *buenos días*. Our once-a-week Saturday flight to the Falklands had originated in Chile but called en route at Rio Gallegos in Argentina to pick up war veterans and their families. I recognised this family as one of those groups and guessed that the father (or one of his brothers) must have been among the largely conscripted Argentine soldiers caught up in the 1982 conflict. I had understood from one of the islanders who was there at the time that the soldiers had been told they were liberators and were disappointed not to find the Falklanders cheering them in the streets.

It is impossible to visit the Falklands without considering that vexed question of where sovereignty rightly lies. Perhaps unsurprisingly, the Argentines view these islands, so close to their own shores – at least in comparison to Britain's, 8,000 miles away – as the object of colonial usurpation. In their eyes, las Malvinas, as they call them, are indisputably Argentinian. But this is of course disputed by the British government, and on three grounds: one distinctly weak, one moderately convincing and one ultimately compelling. The weak argument is historic discovery and settlement, where there are in reality a number of rival claimants. The moderately convincing argument is that the islands have been under settled British administration since 1833. This sounds like a conflation of de facto and de jure – that might has become right. But there does come a point when we accept that the existing order should prevail simply because it has been the existing order for so long. For example, no one seriously suggests that the land sequestrations at the time of the Norman Conquest of Britain should be reversed. That was a thousand years ago. Is the century and three quarters that the Falklands have been British sufficient to enshrine sovereignty? Perhaps; perhaps not.

The ultimately compelling argument, though, is the principle of self-determination. A referendum in 2013 confirmed what everybody pretty much knew already. When asked to indicate whether or not they wished to remain an Overseas Territory of the UK, 92 per cent of the eligible population turned out to vote. Of those, 99.8 per cent (1,513 people) responded 'yes'; only three people voted 'no'. Two independent international organisations monitored the process and endorsed its fairness. It's hard to argue with such an overwhelming democratic consensus.

Of course, the same argument does not easily apply to South Georgia. It has no permanent population to determine its own sovereignty. On the other hand, the Argentine claim is weaker, because the islands are much further (1,300 miles) from its shores. Ultimately Britain's continued claim to South Georgia must surely rest on its record as a conscientious custodian of this sub-Antarctic wilderness.

At 11.41 a.m. on Monday 10 September 2018 we slipped our lines and sailed out of Stanley, bound for the Southern Ocean. I was in a party of twelve on *Pelagic Australis*, a single-masted seventy-four-foot sloop, built in Durban in 2003 and designed specifically for polar waters. The boat had a professional crew of three, although everyone was expected to assist with the sails and the watches. My fellow passengers included our two co-leaders – Stephen Venables, now on his ninth expedition to South Georgia; and the boat's owner, the amply moustachioed Skip Novak, an accomplished yachtsman who had circumnavigated the world five times before becoming an acknowledged expert on polar waters and Antarctic exploration. The remaining seven of us hailed from London, Bristol, Cumbria, Edinburgh, Dundee, Paris and Hong Kong, and would get to know each other rather well over the coming days.

It was calm as we lowered the yacht's retractable keel, set a reefed main and a genoa, and sailed through the protected waters of Stanley Harbour and Port William (the 'Outer Harbour'). On our right, we passed the outlying settlements of Stanley and, looming behind them, higher ground with names familiar from the 1982 conflict such as Tumbledown Hill, Two Sisters and Wireless Ridge. Looming, yes, but not looming that much, because these points, though they were considered strategic in the battle for Stanley, are surprisingly modest in height and extent.

This tranquil start belied what was to come. The next day and night and day again proved a rather grim introduction to the joys of ocean sailing. With a south-east course and a rapidly building northwest wind on our stern, we made a healthy eight knots, but at the cost of a stomach-churning roll. Even Skip, with a life at sea behind him, was popping sea-sickness pills like Smarties. The sails had to be trimmed, but nothing could temper the tumultuous sea. When not on watch, we were all driven to our bunks feeling distinctly sorry for ourselves. And as the wind increased to over forty knots, we felt just that little bit sorrier still. There were small doses of comfort: a pod of dolphins leaping at the bow and, cruising above us, a Great Wanderer, the largest of the albatrosses. But they did little to alleviate the long, confined hours feeling nauseous. I reflected ruefully on my invitation to Rosemary to join us for the 'cruise' section of the trip. She wisely rejected the idea out of hand. Had she accepted, I would have heard the end of it only in the divorce courts!

In the early hours of Wednesday, the wind gradually dropped. We swapped the small staysail for the larger yankee before that in turn gave way to the still larger genoa. It was not long before we needed the engine. The boat steadied a little and we all began to feel a bit better.

Conversation on the watches became more engaged and animated as we started to take less interest in our upset stomachs and more in the backgrounds and endeavours of our companions. My early watches – we were typically two or three hours on and seven off – were led in the main by the petite and quietly-spoken ship's mate, Charlotte, known universally as Charly. She was engaged to our blond-haired and bearded skipper, Edd. The two had met in Scotland, working on a coastal research vessel. But the story that grabbed all our attention was their survival – just – of a record-breaking storm that had struck the Falklands some seven months previously.

The couple were hiking on Cape Dolphin, at the northern tip of East Falkland, when the wind picked up dramatically, forcing them to pitch their tent in the lee of a discarded container, and then within the container itself. As the wind reached 100 knots and more, it flipped the container and tossed it across the unprotected terrain. Edd and Charly were thrown out and both rendered unconscious. When Edd came around, he had no choice but to put Charly back in the container and crawl off for help. He was able to raise the alarm only by breaking into the nearest farmstead and rousing the occupants from their beds. Charly and Edd were both medevacked to Uruguay, Charly with multiple cracked ribs, a broken shoulder, a punctured lung and a partially severed liver. A sobering illustration of the power of the elements in this part of the world.

As the wind dropped on our expedition, we adjusted our course to almost due east in an attempt to get back on track for South Georgia. We crossed the Antarctic Convergence, though there was not much to see other than a heavy mist that might have been caused by the mixing of waters of different temperatures. Still, it seemed significant: a sign of progress.

Thursday brought a further calming of the sea. The sun came out, shadows appeared, and we all reached for our dark glasses. We went to our bunks that evening much happier and with a keen anticipation of landfall the following day.

I took up my watch at 3 a.m., and by the end of it land was already detectable on the radar. Having no intention of missing the first sight of South Georgia, I held to my post and fervently scanned the horizon ahead. Nature offered the first hint of land to come in the form of gentoo penguins surfing through the water, and blue-eyed shags wheeling overhead. It was the sight of these birds, which are only ever seen close to shore, that first convinced Shackleton and his navigator Frank Worsley, aboard *James Caird*, that they were close to South Georgia. Our need for reassurance a century later, in a world with radar and GPS, was rather less pressing than theirs, but the shags were welcome all the same. Then, through the swirling mist, we made out the silhouette of the Willis Islands that sit off the far north-west extremity of South Georgia. Suddenly the ocean, which had been uninterrupted for four days, was filled with rocky islets and icebergs. And sea-birds: more blue-eyed shags, a grey-headed albatross and a variety of petrels, from the large brown giant to the diminutive storm petrel; and later a wandering albatross that soared around the boat, showing off the dazzling white of its massive wings.

Beyond the Willis Islands lay Bird Island, but our attempts to raise the British Antarctic Survey team there on the radio were in vain. Perhaps they didn't expect any visitors so early in the season. We passed to the south of this outpost, but then turned north-east through Bird Island Sound to access the north coast of South Georgia itself. These narrows, filled with mist and harbouring sea arches and other snow-flecked rock formations rising from the foaming ocean, felt like something out of a Nordic fable.

We turned briefly into Right Whale Bay on the north coast of South Georgia, escorted by king penguins that leaped through the water like dolphins. Their compatriots lined the shores in huge numbers, in some cases venturing up the snowy heights behind. There were fur seals, both on land and in the sea. And in the greater distance we could make out the overstuffed-sack-like silhouette of a giant elephant seal. There was a definite sense of arrival.

We had not truly arrived, though, and there was a hint of urgency from our crew. A storm was forecast for the morrow and before nightfall we needed to reach the protection of the island's only permanently occupied settlement, Grytviken, still some six or seven hours away. We motored hard along the north coast. Meanwhile, knowing that we would be able to replenish our water that night, I indulged in my first shower since departing Stanley and some fresh underclothes: a rare treat, and welcome – perhaps not just to me!

I re-emerged from below decks to be greeted by sunshine. The mist had dispersed, revealing in succession the range of peaks that give South Georgia its elevated spine, so different from the popular (and misguided) conception of Antarctica as a flat endless plain. Among the first in line was Stanley Peak (1,263 metres), where Skip had been among the first ascent party. Then Mount Spaaman (1,941 metres) and the aiguille-like Three Brothers (2,040 metres), and in the greater distance Mount Paget, at 2,934 metres the highest point on South Georgia.

As the light began to fail, with darkness hastened by the shadow of those same mountains and many others, we drew into Cumberland Bay. Here the encircling heights and hills – a patchwork of rocky outcrops, snow-filled depressions and occasional tussock grass – conspired to create a protected calm. We checked in first at the government administration post at King Edward Point, docking there at 4.57 p.m. Falklands time.

There was a warm welcome from the smartly uniformed official, Paula, who greeted us as her first vessel of the season. She rightly reinforced the biosecurity concerns and warned us of the potential threat from irate fur seals. Formalities completed, we glided slowly across the bay – through water still enough to reflect the new moon – to our berth for the night at Grytviken. This old whaling station appeared in the last of the light as a silhouette of tangled metal, contorted shapes of a world now past. From 1904 it had been the centre of South Georgia's sealing and whaling industry. That industry exterminated 175,000 whales and innumerable seals in its waters and on its beaches. But all that came to an end when excessive hunting depleted stocks and forced closure in 1965. The ruins remained; the men and women who had lived here were long gone.

Dinner followed and with it a welcome glass of red wine, a pleasant indulgence for a boat that was sensibly dry when underway. And it was a moment for celebration: we had been at sea for four days, six hours and sixteen minutes, during which time our radar had detected a single fishing boat and a handful of icebergs. It had been a unique experience. The first part of our Antarctic odyssey was complete.

We were awake early, eager to explore our new surroundings. Grytviken has a handful of new prefabricated buildings that house a museum and post office, and provide some limited staff accommodation. But from our position on the quay these were obscured by the relics of the whaling era: tanks, silos, hoppers, conveyors, warehouses and even three ships run aground on the beach. They were all a uniform rusted brown, creating a strange harmony of colour, as though installed by a modern artist, a neo-Lowry, bent on conveying the bizarre beauty of this industrial landscape. And it was beautiful. But a stark sort of beauty. There was so much death here in this maritime abattoir.

After breakfast, we visited the small museum. Paula's partner, James, dug out the snow so that we could get in the door. Within were photographs and artefacts of the whaling era, of Shackleton's extraordinary expedition, of the island's wildlife and of the 1982 conflict. That conflict involved a near debacle when the SAS insisted on being landed much too far from their objective, and proved totally unable to cope with the South Georgia weather. They were successfully extracted only after the loss of two helicopters. In contrast, Shackleton and his team's feat two-thirds of a century earlier appeared all the more impressive as we examined the replica of *James Caird*. Battered by an appalling sea, bailing for their lives, unable even to sit up, let alone move around; cold, wet, exhausted and desperately thirsty, they somehow survived the sea crossing in this cramped, leaky craft.

Next door to the museum, James doubled as Postmaster General and furnished South Georgia stamps for our postcards home, which would no doubt arrive long after we had returned. Stamps – much sought after by collectors – are an important source of income for this diminutive sovereign territory.

Three of us strolled around the bay to King Edward Point, passing a solitary gentoo penguin who looked rather lost and lonesome. A family of South Georgia pintail ducks waddled around near the shore, their dull brown plumage enlivened only by their bright yellow beaks. And, to our delight, bobbing here and there were South Georgia pipits, the island's only songbird, once threatened with extinction but now recovering rapidly in the wake of the successful eradication of rats on the island. Added to that were three snow petrels, virgin-white scavengers, and the ubiquitous terns, hovering over the water, poised to strike at any fish that dared near the surface.

We passed the government office and the modern science laboratories, all housed in long prefabs, then upped the pace a bit as we strode through the tussock grass with fur seals barking at us from both sides. At length we reached Hope Point, its panoramic view broken only by the rocky mass of Mount Duse behind. Here Shackleton's men erected a cross in his memory. Shackleton himself is buried on the grassy slopes on the opposite side of the bay. Next to his grave lies that of Frank Wild, his second-in-command, who asked that his body be laid to rest beside that of 'the boss'.

We returned via the church, built in 1913 by the pioneering Norwegian whaler Carl Anton Larsen. Known as the Whalers' Church, it is attractively simple in design, painted white within and without, with just a trace of blue-green to match the bay beyond. Its roof is appropriately modelled on a ship's upturned hull, and the butter-gold cross on its steeple acts as a beacon for all who approach. A small placard informed us that the rector was based in the Falklands and was responsible for one of the largest parishes in the world, covering a span of no less than 900 miles. Visitors were encouraged to ring the church's two bells and so we did, sending our greetings to the local populace, currently doubled in number by the presence of *Pelagic Australis*.

The permanent winter flock comprised nine members of the British Antarctic Survey, two government officials (Paula and her colleague Steve), and Paula's partner James, himself a former head of the station. The most recent signature in the visitors' book was a collective one on behalf of the research ship RRS *Ernest Shackleton*. It was dated 2 June 2018, some four months earlier.

The church also incorporated an extensive library, still used by its parishioners. The titles told something of the interests, dreams and fears of the largely male whaling community of that past era. We were particularly taken with *Rapture in Rags*, *The Sinister Wife*, *Inviting Fingers* and *The Reluctant Hussey* – a perfect counterpoise to other works of a more liturgical nature.

That evening, the neighbours – both of them – called round for a drink. Although ours was the only boat to have arrived so far that season, there was one other sailing yacht there already in the harbour. It was the twenty-eight-foot *Wanderer III*, built in 1952 and home to a delightfully eccentric couple in their fifties, the silver-bearded German/Danish Thies Matzen and his graceful Swedish wife, Kicki Ericson. They had been helping to monitor the rodent eradication programme and to restore the wooden windows in the Whalers' Church, the church in which they had been married twenty years previously. The work had taken longer than expected and they had been caught by the onset of winter. Having no radar, they had not dared risk running the gauntlet of the icebergs and were forced to sit it out in Grytviken until spring.

During the night we got a taste of the katabatic wind that South Georgia is famed for. It whistled down from the heights above and funnelled through the derelict and twisted whaling machinery as if through organ pipes: an eerie, mournful harmony. It was a warning, too, because it was strong enough to blow off a hatch cover.

We awoke to gently falling snow. Notwithstanding, this was our opportunity to test our gear on the hill. Beside our crew of three, there were nine group members split into two teams. The skiing or 'expedition' team, of which I was a member, was headed by Stephen Venables and Skip Novak. It included Stephen Reid, owner of a climbing store in Cumbria and an experienced mountaineer with many first ascents to his name in the UK, Peru and Greenland; and Kirsty Maguire, an architect from Dundee. Kirsty, an impressively fit ultra-fell-runner, was a member of the Scottish Mountain Rescue team and had just returned from ski touring in Arctic Norway.

The four-person support team was with us for day trips and to enjoy the wildlife and atmosphere in this wildest and most atmospheric of places. It also brought considerable mountaineering ability, but was unsuited for longer excursions due to lack of sufficient experience on skis. In particular, Colin Knowles, a retired IT manager from Bristol, had climbed in the UK for much of his life and served on various bodies for the British Mountaineering Council. Colin was my room-mate – or more accurately berth-mate, because our twin bunks were located in a corridor. When I later discovered he was a member of Red Rope, the UK's only communist climbing club, I couldn't help but exclaim, 'They've shacked me up with a commie!' Fortunately, Colin took it well and we became firm friends. Kinman Chung was also an experienced mountaineer, being a rock-climbing instructor and a veteran of the Seven Summits, including Everest. Against this pair, I felt a bit of a fraud being part of the expedition team, but of course an ability to ski competently off-piste was of paramount importance in this snow-bound part of the world. Meanwhile, a third South African crew member, Kirsten Neuschäfer, the half-French, half-Swedish photographer Jonas Lam, and Skip's girlfriend Jennifer Coombs, a super-organised and upbeat ex-actress and High Sheriff of Dorset, completed a varied and engaging group.

Skip spent the day with Jennifer, but the remaining four members of the expedition team set their sights on a 600-metre ridge between the various peaks of Mount Narval. This involved skinning up an initially gentle slope that became steeper and icier as we progressed. This form of ski mountaineering requires the use of skins (originally seal skins, now synthetic) that are attached with a temporary adhesive to the base of the ski and allow it to glide uphill but prevent it from sliding back downhill. These skins can be supplemented with couteaux: ski crampons that sit underneath each foot and provide a similar function to the skins but with added bite. On this steepening ground, I was soon using my couteaux and was hugely impressed that our fearless leader Stephen V seemed to manage happily without. Only later did I discover that it wasn't by choice – he just didn't have any! Eventually we were obliged to trade our skis for regular crampons and axes. The two Stephens and I rotated the lead as we kicked steps up to and then left along the ridge. The going here got more serious. We were without either a rope or our second ice tools, a strong wind was blowing across the ridge and a fall to the left would have been a fatal one. I was out front and waited for Stephen V to catch up. We conferred and decided enough was enough. We would enjoy the view from the ridge where we were.

And quite a view it was. The falling snow had long given way to sunshine. To one side we could see the route we had just climbed, right down to the deep-blue water of Cumberland East Bay. The red-and-white prefabs of King Edward Point were just visible beyond the surrounding cliffs that obscured neighbouring Grytviken. To the other side, a succession of snowy ridges led the eye to the more distant, but equally impressive, Cumberland West Bay, similarly encircled by snowy peaks. It was easy to see why the Norwegian whalers and sealers had felt so at home here, the coastline being deeply indented everywhere in the manner of the fjords.

Our first attempts at Antarctic downhill skiing were not entirely encouraging. Kirsty descended the upper slopes in crampons with her skis on her pack, and no doubt rather enjoyed the sight of the two Stephens and I making fools of ourselves, struggling and failing to ski the breakable crust. In fairness, this half-frozen snow is some of the most difficult to negotiate on skis. Once the skis have broken through the surface, they are effectively locked in a set of tramlines. There is little option other than to continue in a straight line. The problem is that you cannot traverse forever. Eventually there is a moment of reckoning when the skier simply must turn and, when it comes, it is rarely a pretty sight. Mercifully the breakable crust was short-lived. But in its stead came equally unforgiving ice, which did little to improve our performance. Then, at last, the surface softened and we enjoyed some fine turns on the lower slopes, with morale and dented pride at least partially restored by the time we reached Grytviken and the boat.

The following morning, with further fresh snow falling, we motored slowly out of Cumberland Bay and made a modest eight-kilometre trip south-east along the coast, before entering a narrow channel to take refuge in the small and almost perfectly circular Cobblers Cove. Having transferred ship-to-shore in the Zodiac (inflatable tender), we clambered around the cliffs and down through the thick, snow-encrusted tussock grass. Via a narrow isthmus, we arrived at a boulder-shaped land mass somewhat incongruously named Long Point, it being neither long nor pointed. This causeway was all that separated the cove from its larger neighbour, Godthul – another of those Norwegian-sounding names that are such a feature of South Georgia's topography.

With the sea accessible on either side, this was a particularly populous wildlife spot. The blubbery bulk of a male elephant seal with its preposterous proboscis lay motionless on the beach; bewhiskered fur seals sat alert, seemingly scanning the horizon; and a teeming crush of gentoo penguins stood somewhat absurdly to attention as though in a guard of honour. One penguin, though, was definitely not on parade. It had clearly been attacked by a leopard seal and half its neck had been eaten away. Its prospects did not look promising.

Back on *Pelagic Australis*, we faced our own challenge as the wind picked up again, threatening the boat. We needed to back up the anchor with a shore line. Our first attempt ended when the cable parted, and by the time the boat was properly secured, twilight was upon us. We mounted an anchor-watch throughout the night. This was one of the best-protected anchorages on South Georgia and, with suitable diligence, we were safe enough. But the first hints of anxiety were emerging as to when, and indeed whether, we would get ashore properly to mount our expedition. The leading mountaineering book on Antarctica describes South Georgia as 'stormy, rugged, windswept, formidable'.[24] It was living up to all that.

Another day in the same anchorage allowed a pleasant tour of the heights above and some fine skiing in descent, but did nothing to alleviate the growing concern. The next day opened with fine weather. However, a strong easterly was forecast. We motored ten kilometres or so further down the coast to an inlet called Ocean Harbour, an old whalers' bay, the sole relic being the rusting wreck of a three-masted vessel festooned with cormorants.

This jumping-off point furnished a first taste of a real South Georgia journey. Four of us climbed, on skis and skins, across a broad snow field, then up bone-hard ice, past a turquoise-blue mountain lake, to reach a precarious arête. There, out in front, I led the way, unroped and poised gingerly between an overhanging cornice on my right and a steeper-than-I-would-have-liked slope of sheet ice on my left. Had I fallen to either side, my halt would have been neither soon nor elegant. To make matters worse I was still on skis, skins and couteaux. I dearly wished I'd switched earlier to axe and crampons and secured my skis on my pack. But it was too late now. Any attempt to do that on so pronounced a ridge would have courted disaster. Instead, I shuffled along between this Scylla and Charybdis, fighting for a grip, until I reached the relative security of some rocks and could at last make the change.

Half our party left their skis there and continued without, but Stephen V and I persevered, carrying them on our backs up a further ice slope to a small col that separated the two aiguille-like rocky summits of Black Peak (805 metres). We weren't sure which summit was the higher, so Stephen climbed one while I and the others climbed its twin. Ours proved the true summit, but Stephen's, being without doubt the more elegant, stole the show.

As is so often the case, the real excitement was on the way down. It was one of those skiing situations where to fall was not an acceptable option; to lose a ski even less so, for a dropped ski would not have stopped much short of the sea. Against all the usual principles, I jacked my bindings up to the maximum. This of course meant that, if I fell, then my skis would not detach, and I risked a wrenched knee or worse. But that seemed better than the alternatives. Happily, we descended without incident, first in sunshine down the terrain we had climbed and then at dusk down the broad and shallow Sörling Valley, rejoining the boat on the shore of Cumberland East Bay and thus completing a traverse of the peninsula. The ski descent was made all the more memorable by the view down that valley and across the water to the mountain range beyond, which featured, at its very centre, the island's highest peak, Mount Paget.

Our final leg by boat back to King Edward Point involved navigating myriad small icebergs, blown in by the building easterly. By the time we woke the next morning, the scene was Shackletonesque. Our boat was becoming locked in by the endless slabs of floating ice, which were now freezing to each other – a mosaic of as-yet-unconnected pieces being rapidly crafted by the wind and cold into a final fixed artwork. Neither our friends from *Wanderer III* nor anyone else from the base at King Edward Point had ever seen so much ice in the bay, even in the depths of winter.

Still, it didn't seem to bother the seals. I counted three different species in the bay that morning: an enormous male elephant seal, grunting vociferously; a leopard seal, laid out on an ice floe having presumably overindulged in fresh penguin; and the ubiquitous and ferocious fur seals, one of which had to be warded off with a ski pole.

The day afforded us a new South Georgia experience: being caught out on the hill in Antarctic weather. Five of us made a day-hike from Grytviken over the Thatcher Peninsula, named of course after the British Prime Minister at the time of the 1982 conflict. Conditions steadily worsened. Our return route, skinning up a gully into the full force of a wind that drove snow horizontally into our faces, demonstrated what it meant to battle with the elements in these parts. The Thatcher Peninsula gave us the full handbagging, but mercifully our journey was a short one and soon we were back in the warm protection of *Pelagic Australis*.

Just as Shackleton's men on *Endurance* made the most of their icy incarceration, so did we at King Edward Point. There was no football on the ice for us, but we were invited by the resident British Antarctic Survey team to tour their facility and join them in their bar for drinks. The team included two scientists plus the head of station, two marine engineers or 'boaties' (as they described themselves), a mechanical engineer, a chef and a doctor. This group also lent support to the other British Antarctic Survey team on Bird Island, where there was just one generalist engineer looking after three scientists.

I chatted to one of the scientists, Vicky, a marine biologist monitoring the local krill, icefish and Patagonia toothfish populations as part of the fisheries-management policy. A tall, attractive woman in her early thirties, she had not left South Georgia in two years. Somewhat in jest, she claimed she had forgotten 'the art of conversation'. Those who choose these remote assignments are obviously a special kind of people, but they are more numerous than one might think. Vicky told us there had been 168 applicants for her role. Such an environment requires team members to take on multiple functions. For example, Paula, the government officer, was also the manager of the museum shop, the registrar for marriages (cost: £400 per hitch) and the chief of police – complete with her own gaol. When Paula announced she would show us her police uniform and disappeared off to her bedroom to find it, well, we were not quite certain what was coming. But sure enough, it was the genuine article. Whether she had a clerical cassock and collar as well I rather doubt, but she was certainly a woman of many talents.

We awoke on our fourth day in the pack ice to find at last salvation. The wind had dropped, the large bergs blocking the inner bay's entrance had gone, and the ice immediately around the boat was breaking up rapidly. Departure, however, was hardly instant. The frozen shore lines had to be dug out from under deep snow, forced reluctantly through the boat's cleats and coiled as best their contorted shapes would allow. When Stephen V and I hoisted the mainsail, we wished we'd donned our climbing helmets, as chunks of ice dropped heavily around us, released from the mast and canvas above. Still, there was real relief and excitement as we waved goodbye to our neighbours on *Wanderer III*, and at 8.45 a.m. at last broke free. It had all been a little too closely reminiscent of dear old Ernest.

We sailed south-east down the coast, past our previous anchorages at Cobblers Cove and Ocean Harbour and on into new territory. As we pushed on further south, the wintry feel became even wintrier, with snow and ice increasingly blotting out the tussock grass. After eight hours, we pulled into Drygalski Fjord, the major arterial waterway at this corner of the island. From there we accessed one of its tributaries, Larsen Harbour, which despite its name turned out to be very much a fjord and had no sign of human habitation, past or present.

We had been prepared for something special, Thies and Kicki having declared this their favourite place on South Georgia. We were not disappointed. Larsen was pristinely beautiful. The steep cliffs, plastered in ice, fell sheer into the stillest of calm waters. Almost-perfect reflections left the viewer uncertain as to what was up and what was down. Meanwhile, on the shore, five female Weddell seals, the most southerly of the seal family, suckled their pups.

But there was work to be done. All our gear needed to be prepared for a full expedition-landing the next day. I ran through my equipment for the nth time and placed it in dry bags, ready to be transferred ashore and packed into a pulk.

Next day, we weighed anchor at 8 a.m. and motored around the remainder of the island's south-east peninsula. South Georgia was only properly named and put on the map by Captain James Cook in 1775. He sailed down the north-east coast, as we had just done, hoping that he had discovered a new continent in the Southern Ocean. As he rounded this peninsula and found himself sailing once more north-west, he realised that he had discovered only an island. Accordingly, he christened the peninsula Cape Disappointment.

We, however, were in no way disappointed by what we found, which to our surprise and delight was a flat, calm sea, almost unheard of on this wild, little-visited, southern coast. Three hours after leaving Larsen, we dropped anchor off Trollhul, a broad, open bay, exposed to everything the weather gods might send. But, in this instance, they sent nothing. We gazed across the tranquil dark-blue waters to the lighter aquamarine of two glaciers, one tumbling to the very shoreline – blue meeting blue – the other curtailed, hanging high above us with just the vestiges of a moraine carved in the rock below.

KEY

- - - *Pelagic Australis'* route

◄ Start of traverse at Trollhul Bay

△ Mount Dow

We wasted no time and with half a dozen trips in the Zodiac had all our equipment ashore, cached a safe distance from the enormous male elephant seals that were already staking their claims on the beach. We divided the communal gear – tents, gas stoves, fuel, food, ropes, pickets, ice saws, repair kit and emergency equipment – between our five pulks.

Back on board *Pelagic Australis* we ran through the expedition itinerary one last time. South Georgia is roughly 100 miles long, twenty miles wide at its narrowest point, and oriented north-west to south-east. It thus has two long coasts. The north-east coast, where all the settlements (past and present) are, and down which we had just sailed, is the comparatively benign coast. 'Comparatively' is an important qualification, because it was on this same coast that we had recently been buffeted by forty-knot katabatic winds and trapped by pack ice for four days! Nonetheless, it is generally milder than the much-less-visited south-west coast where we were now at anchor. The mountain interior divides neatly into two ranges separated by the Ross Pass. In the north-west is the now relatively well-trodden Allardyce Range, first crossed by Shackleton a century ago; and, in the south-east, the road less travelled, the Salvesen Range.

Our plan was to traverse South Georgia from south to north at this southerly end of the island. This would involve crossing the entire Salvesen Range from Trollhul on the south coast to St Andrews Bay on the north coast, skiing or skinning over nine glaciers and surmounting seven cols. For this we were allowing a maximum of ten days and were carrying food and fuel accordingly. We were not going where no man had gone before (boldly or otherwise). But we were going where very few men (or women) had been before – probably fewer than thirty of them. Clearly we would need to be self-sufficient. There would be no way of getting further supplies to us once we departed – and no prospect of a rescue were we to get into trouble. There would be no 'Beam me up, Scottie' on this trip.

The five of us got ashore the next morning without incident. Our immediate objective was to climb out of the bay and establish ourselves on the plateau of the Graae Glacier above. It was too steep for skis and skins, so we strapped these to our pulks, donned crampons, divided our gear into two roughly equal loads and ferried it upward. I was the last off the shore, but the first to top out with my second load, largely because of a perhaps foolhardy willingness to use my empty pulk as a toboggan between the lifts.

Reunited after three hours, we all roped up and, led by Skip, skinned north steadily up the glacier to our first col at just below 600 metres, before dropping slightly down on to a second glacier, the Harmer. Snowfall had given way to sunshine and a view once more to the sea. It was 3.30 p.m. and time to pitch camp. But only once we had probed the terrain for hidden crevasses did we dare step out of our skis, which of course spread the bodyweight much more effectively than boots.

This was not a place to chance the weather. We had two Terra Nova tents, built for these conditions with inner and outer shells, double poles and valances – canvas flaps that extended from the tent horizontally over the ground. We loaded the valances with large blocks of snow, sawn from a snow pit, to prevent the wind driving up between the flysheet and the inner tent. We then pegged the whole thing down with pickets, ice axes and skis. It was as robust a construction as was possible in such circumstances. Stephen V, Kirsty and I took one tent; Skip and Stephen Reid the other.

Then, a couple of domestic setbacks. First, we discovered that the cutlery and crockery bag for our tent had been left behind. No spoons, forks, cups or bowls for this ten-day expedition. We improvised, using food containers as bowls and broken bits of plastic for spoons, which was a source of much dark humour over the coming days. Many Pythonesque references were made along the lines of 'Spoons! Luxury! You was lucky. We didn't have spoons … !' The second setback was that, despite extensive testing at home, Stephen Reid's and my Thermarest mattresses were no sooner inflated than they started to leak. That meant some cold nights to come for both of us.

It snowed heavily overnight and continued to do so in the morning – to the extent that we couldn't move on. Instead, we built an elaborate igloo as a latrine. It was a good team-building exercise, but it was still a full day lost to the weather. It was not to be the last.

By 10 a.m. the next day we were able to strike camp and were away at midday. It was a long, hard grind up to a second col at around 750 metres and then flat as we contoured on to the Novosilski Glacier with another splendid view on our left down to the southern shore. The eight centimetres of fresh snow that had fallen during the preceding thirty-six hours made the going tough. Even with a redistribution of the loads, breaking trail with the lead pulk was a strenuous business.

We pitched camp again and, as we did each night, contacted the boat by satellite phone for a weather forecast. It was distinctly discouraging: high winds for many days to come. Notwithstanding that, we were away the next morning by 8.15 a.m. We took turns breaking trail, but in the still-soft snow it was agonisingly slow progress. By 1 p.m. we had climbed only forty metres and covered just four kilometres. Ahead of us still lay a long climb up a crevassed glacier to reach the Spenceley Col, at 1,250 metres the highest point on our planned traverse. There was no prospect of our making that or anywhere close to that before nightfall, so we elected to pitch camp where we were. While the others put up the tents, Stephen Reid and I did a first ferry of gear up half the route ahead, dumping a cache, which we marked with wands and a GPS fix. That was the most we could manage for the day ...

... and the next day, and the day after that. We spent two and a half days and three nights without moving an inch. There were occasional periods when we could get out of the tent. One such allowed us to build a protecting perimeter wall ahead of an accurately forecast further deterioration in the weather. But, in general, we were trapped beneath the canvas as more snow fell, often driven horizontally across the glacier by the strong winds. Outside we could hear the sound of avalanches cascading down the neighbouring peaks, especially from nearby Mount Paterson.

Our second full day in the tent was my fifty-ninth birthday. My present from the weather gods was the strongest wind yet. Kirsty went outside at one point to dig out the tent and better secure our kit. Without her additional, albeit modest, weight inside, I thought we might be carried away! Still, we got through another night. By this stage, though, I was wearing every stitch of clothing I had. Within my sleeping and bivvy bags, I wore socks and down booties, underpants, thin and thick long johns, short- and long-sleeve thermal shirts, two fleeces, belay jacket and full 6,000-metre duvet; plus balaclava and wool hat as well as hoods from the jacket, duvet and sleeping bag. Even so, I was cold.

Mercifully we awoke on the third day to better weather. More than better: beautiful. The sun rose over Mount Paterson and streaked down the fresh carpet of snow on the Novosilski Glacier, capturing in turn the adjacent summits – the pointed top of Mount Baume, the as-yet-unclimbed twin peaks of Mount Dow, and the more distant, looming mass of Mount Carse, the highest mountain in the range and first climbed by our leader, Stephen V – before at last illuminating the shoreline and the sea below.

We did not dally. We were away at 8 a.m. I took the lead pulk and broke trail. Crucially, the recent snow had now consolidated and the surface had hardened, making progress very much easier than it had been three days previously. In little over an hour we had recovered the cache. But as we approached the col, the weather closed in again, forcing us to rely on GPS and compass bearings with orders – 'left, right, right again' and so on – barked from the rear to those at the front. During our meanderings, Stephen V felt his skis sink into a crevasse. He was able to extract himself. Still, it was a concern. Falling into a crevasse is never welcome, but it is especially daunting when you are strapped to a pulk the weight of a man.

As we neared the col, we were met by a violent headwind and, with the pulks pulling us back, were barely able to make ground. We stopped at the col only long enough to strip off our skins and put our skis into downhill mode. Then, still in a white-out, we snow-ploughed tentatively down the other side, making sure we all stayed in close touch. We were now on the Spenceley, the glacial highway at the very heart of the Salvesen Range – not that we could see any of it beyond a few metres ahead.

By 1.45 p.m. we were down to 1,000 metres. The glacier flattened as we descended and we had to pole to maintain momentum in the fresh snow. The wind dropped and to some extent our guard dropped with it. A feeling almost of boredom set in. And then all hell broke loose. In a matter of minutes, we went from near calm to a relentless fifty-knot wind, with occasional gusts well in excess of that, driving snow into our faces. We could barely see, barely speak and, for a moment, barely think. There was no question of going any further. The body heat was already draining from us. We needed to make camp there and then. Attempting to erect the tents, though, in such a wind and on an open glacier would have been risky. A half-erected tent is very much like a sail and, even with five of us, it was far from certain that we would be able to hold on to it.

We set about building a protecting wall of ice blocks. Our initial efforts might have been quite comical had the situation not been so serious. Unable to see, we staggered around, frequently losing our balance and easily felled by a sudden gust. I was knocked to the ground a dozen times. There was a point when I thought 'If this gets any worse, any worse at all, we are in deep trouble', but soon enough the team settled into the task. Skip and Stephen Reid sawed blocks of ice, while Stephen V and I conveyed these to Kirsty, who as our resident architect constructed a double-layer wall to shoulder height. With that completed, we were able to get one tent up and cram all five of us in. It was cramped, but none of us cared much: we were safe for now. That's all that mattered. Stephen V described it as 'the first "full-on" I've had in thirty years', which, coming from him, was quite something. I was feeling pretty cold by now and had lost sensation in my feet, but it was nothing that a hot drink, a foot massage and squeezing five people into a single tent couldn't put right!

We emerged the next day somewhat battle-weary. It was a recovery day. The wind and snow had abated, but a white-out ruled against striking camp. Instead, we erected the second tent, dug a proper latrine, and got some much-needed rest.

A clear blue sky greeted us the following morning and a mesmerising view down the Spenceley Glacier, flanked by a succession of mountain peaks and nunataks (rocky outcrops), to the iceberg-strewn Southern Ocean beyond. Overhead flew perfectly camouflaged snow petrels, the only birds to venture this far into the interior. It took some hours to dig out the tents, but after that our progress was rapid. We glided on our skis down this impressive glacier, where no more than two or perhaps three dozen people had ever been before. Soon we were back on our skins, climbing again, this time up the Brøgger Glacier to reach a ridge of nunataks guarding the entrance to the Ross Pass.

Here a dilemma presented itself. We had been going no more than three hours but, rolling into the pass from the north, we could see a broad, heavy, sinister bank of cloud. The Ross Pass is notoriously the windiest place on South Georgia and thus, by implication, one of the windiest places on earth. It is not somewhere to get caught in a storm. If we committed to the pass, we would have to get through it and down the other side, but that might be on our hands and knees. Or it might be not at all. We went for caution. With an aching sense of disappointment, we pitched camp there among the nunataks. It was a tough decision, but in so remote a place, Plan A was survival through self-reliance and there was no Plan B. We couldn't take a chance.

That afternoon we congratulated ourselves on our decision as some of the strongest winds yet battered the tents, but when there was a lull the following morning, we decided to go for it. The wind was driving left-to-right across our direction of travel, rather than into our faces, and it was a north wind, which in these parts is the warm one, blowing down from the equatorial zone. Out in front, breaking trail up to the pass itself, I rather enjoyed the sense of adventure and drama it created, the mountain peaks either side drifting in and out of view in the swirling mist.

As we breasted the pass just after noon, the mist eclipsed any remaining visibility. Once more we had to resort to GPS and compass bearings as we skied cautiously down the other side. Stephen V, now in the lead, did his best to maintain a course, while at the same time avoiding any obvious holes. Then suddenly he vanished. I probed forward and found him sprawled eight metres below me. He had fallen into a crevasse – luckily, one filled with snow. His pulk had inevitably followed him in, landing on top of him. His skis were sprawled everywhere. For a moment – it seemed a long moment – he lay there motionless. Then there were reassuring grunts of indignation. No harm done, but a salutary warning. We all roped up.

When eventually the mist lifted a little, we found we had wandered into an extensive crevasse field with gaping holes on all sides. There was nothing to do but retreat – carefully. At this point, stretching too far over my skis to retrieve a rope, I sustained a silly injury, fracturing a rib on my right side. It didn't actually inhibit my movements but was an unwelcome irritation for the rest of the trip – and for some time thereafter!

We had hoped to find somewhere less exposed to the forecast westerly wind before nightfall, but we couldn't stagger on blindly over this terrain. There was no choice but to make our sixth camp where we were, out there in the middle of the Ross Glacier. At least we were down at 300 metres rather than up in the pass, which was at twice that height. And we had covered over ten kilometres that day: a decent distance in such conditions.

The next day, again without visibility and surrounded by chasms, we couldn't see our route through to reach our next objective, the foot of the Webb Glacier. We weren't lost, we reassured ourselves; we just didn't know exactly where we were. In this age of GPS and detailed maps, this might seem strangely incompetent, but there were two factors that made things less straightforward than they might appear. First, we had no detailed map. We had the most detailed map available, a recently updated one from the British Antarctic Survey – but for the remote southern half of South Georgia this was only 1:200,000. To put that in context, most mountaineers rely on a 1:25,000 map; to cover the same area, you would need sixty-four of these! Rather than five-metre or ten-metre contours, we had only 100-metre contours. And GPS is only as good as the map you are plotting it on. Second, we were on a glacier, a moving body of ice that changes from year to year and, in this time of global warming, that means changing quite a lot. Knowing your compass bearing is of limited value if your route is blocked by an unbridgeable crevasse. Indeed, there was a possibility that there simply wasn't a route through to reach the Webb Glacier – at least, not one that was navigable with heavy pulks. As an alternative, we discussed abandoning our attempt to reach St Andrews Bay and simply descending the Ross Glacier all the way to its bottom, where it meets the shore at Royal Bay, also on the north coast. But, if anything, this looked even more crevassed and complicated and would probably have required us to jettison most of our equipment. Plus, there was no surety that the boat could get in close enough to extract us from Royal Bay.

We had budgeted for ten days' food and fuel and were already beyond that. We were down to dehydrated mashed potato and what looked to me like birdseed, not an appetising prospect either singly or in combination. The whole thing was threatening to develop into what climbers call an 'epic', although I prefer the term 'situation', which I find goes down rather better at home.

Various reconnaissance trips were mounted without success, until the two Stephens went off for one final effort. They found a route through to the Webb, albeit one that would require us to cross a deep snow-filled crevasse and somehow get the pulks up the other side. By this point, though, it was too late to move that day. We were committed to another night out there on the glacier.

A 3.15 a.m. alarm opened what was our twelfth day in the Salvesen Range. Encouragingly, stars lit the sky – but it was windy. We lowered the pulks into the crevasse and then hauled them with ropes up the other side. That gave access to a gentler snow slope which we traversed and then descended – some of us on skis, others on foot – to reach the shallow plane of the Webb Glacier. I stood for a moment, admiring the magnificent vista down to Royal Bay, with the snow and ice of the glacier reaching all the way to the deep-blue Southern Ocean. It was our first view of the island's north-east coast in twelve days.

The harmony of the moment was rudely broken. My eyes suddenly became riveted to my left ski. The skin had detached and was gone. I had to control a rising sense of panic. We had no spares and, without a skin, I would seriously struggle to overcome the final pass that lay between us and safety. I removed my skis and carefully retraced my steps. Desperately I searched for the lost skin. Fifteen minutes up the hill, I spotted just a few centimetres of the synthetic material poking through the snow. Such was the sense of relief, and so fired up was I as a result, that I broke trail for almost the entire climb up to the final pass.

We reached the last col at 12.45 p.m. in perfect sunshine. Nothing could stop us now. We took off our skins, locked our skis into downhill mode and swept down the wide, undulating, somewhat fairy-tale-like Cook Glacier, meandering between snowy ridges and Obelix-sized boulders to reach the very shore of St Andrews Bay. We arrived just as the sun was at its most attractive trajectory, illuminating the world's largest colony of nesting king penguins – all 400,000 of them. They represent another of

South Georgia's great success stories, since in 1925 hunting had reduced their numbers to just 1,100. Quite a recovery! We picked our way carefully between the formally attired adults on the one side and their fluffy brown balls of chicks on the other, and down to the water's edge where huge male elephant seals were preparing to battle it out for partners. To our surprise we found *two* yachts at anchor. In addition to *Pelagic Australis* there was a smaller ketch, *Santa Maria Australis*, temporary home to a film crew jointly contracted by the BBC and PBS. For producers of nature documentaries, this bay is one of the star attractions anywhere in the world. And quite a place to end a ski tour!

Friends and champagne greeted us on the beach, and a splendid dinner followed on board ship. Of course, the journey was not yet complete. There was still a five-day sail back to the Falklands, but we had made it coast-to-coast through one of the remotest mountain regions in the world.

Some time later ...

It seemed a long while since I had sat on a sofa, especially a sofa as elegant as this one. As I attempted to achieve the delicate balance between getting comfortably settled and yet not slouching uncouthly, one of several uniformed waitresses offered me a cup of tea and a scone topped with clotted cream and jam. A little juggling act followed, where I crossed my legs – still clad in climbing trousers and appended with fell-running boots – attempted my most sophisticated and urbane pose with cup, saucer and scone, and failed miserably. My host, Nigel Phillips, in jacket and tie, and his wife Emma, equally smartly attired for the occasion, seemed immune to these complications as they took the competing demands of tea, scone and conversation in their well-practised stride.

My fellow travellers and I – all twelve of us – were in their magnificent drawing room, carpeted and sofa'd from wall to wall. It gave on to an equally glorious conservatory, the length of the house, which had an uninterrupted view to the sea. The ceiling was reinforced to support a full-sized snooker table in the room above. Our hospitable hosts filled us in on the local scene, while their Labrador, Gibson, exercised a level of self-restraint in respect of the scones only rarely witnessed in the canine species. It could have been a country manor house on the Isle of Wight. But it wasn't. Our host held two roles. He was both the Governor of the Falkland Islands and Her Majesty's Commissioner for South Georgia and the South Sandwich Islands. We were back in Stanley, and guests at Government House.

Having been generously fêted there, we began an evening of celebration. First up was a pint of warm draft beer at the 'Vic' pub, the 'Vic' being short not for Victoria but for Victory. Union Jack bunting hung everywhere. The Gents' displayed a (second) toilet seat mounted on the wall, framing a photograph of General Galtieri, the Argentine dictator at the time of the 1982 conflict. The caption underneath was not flattering.

After that, another celebratory drink and dinner at Stanley's finest hotel, where I went for the Fish 'n' Chips, that being suitably British in this place which was, after all, more British that Britain itself. Having travelled the seven continents, it seemed fitting to have ended up somewhere at one and the same time so far from and so near to home.

NOT-SO-FINAL THOUGHTS

I trust by this stage that you, the reader, are seething with irate indignation. I do hope so. 'Those routes aren't the finest in the world, or even close!' I hear you exclaim. 'What about X and Y and Z?' Excellent. If we didn't all have differing views on what makes a great climb, what on earth would we talk about in the pub (or refuge)? Wherever we are and whatever we are drinking – whether the beer be warm and brown or cold and pale or cloudy and white – half the fun of a climb is the post-match analysis. So please indulge your indignation. Let it fume away.

Looking back, I don't suppose any keen mountaineer ever presented his or her spouse with a weaker excuse for multiple wonderful climbing trips all over the world. Even the most casual reader among you will by now have worked out that the whole thing is little more than a delightful ruse for having a very good time. It is to be thoroughly recommended.

What it most definitely has not been is a box-ticking exercise. Indeed, if anything, these climbs have been less about endings than beginnings. First, they have been a reason (Rosemary would say 'excuse') to do things (she would add 'reckless and unnecessary' things) that I might otherwise never have done. And, beyond that, rather than being a conclusion in themselves, they have often led to further excursions of a related kind. My continued interest in aid climbing, fired initially by the climb on the *Nose*, is an obvious example. As are my repeated trips to the Alps. And, throughout this period, I have never ceased drawing huge pleasure from cragging on my native British rock.

A key characteristic of these climbs, taken together, has been their variety. We live in an age of specialisation. 'Focus' is so often the watchword. But these routes were chosen in part to achieve the very opposite. They are deliberately diverse: 'trad' rock climbing in Kenya, aid climbing on El Cap, ice climbing on Alpamayo, Himalayan expedition-style climbing on Ama Dablam, mixed climbing on the Eiger and Aoraki/ Mount Cook, and ski mountaineering in South Georgia. Some may say that such a broad spread comes at the cost of excellence, but I would rather be a broad-minded incompetent amateur than a narrowly-focused one. My search has not been to achieve a 'first', but to find another kind of challenge, of satisfaction, of fun. The only barriers I have sought to break through have been ones personal to me.

Was it necessary to visit all the world's seven continents? Perhaps not. And yet, without that further diversity, something again would have been lost. Part of the pleasure of it all was seeking out routes – locations, approaches and climbs – that, I hoped, might capture something of the natural environment and mountain culture of these very different continents.

So, where from here? Job done? Rather like parenting, the job is never done. That same year, 2018, in which I was completing my seventh route in Antarctica, I also climbed for the first time in the Austrian Alps. After a preparatory assault of the North Face of the Hochfeiler in the Zillertal range, we turned our sights on our main objective, the Pallavicini Couloir on the Grossglockner. This arrow-straight couloir of glistening snow and ice steepens to seventy degrees before it tops out with geometric precision between the twin peaks of Austria's highest mountain. The simplicity of this line and its situation is surely close to aesthetic perfection. As we climbed it, I couldn't help but wonder whether this might, after all, be the finest route in Europe, finer even than the North Face of the Eiger. The 1938 Route on the latter is the ultimate exemplar of the complex, winding route up a mountain. The Pallavicini Couloir is the very opposite.

So, which ranks foremost: winding ingenuity or ascetic simplicity? And could there be other routes still better than both of these? Difficult to say. I guess the only solution is to go and check ... But how to explain to my ever-patient wife?

REFERENCES

1. Simpson, Joe, *The Beckoning Silence* (Vintage, 2002), p.281

2. Clough, Ian, 'Eigerwand, 1962', *Alpine Journal* Volume 68 (1963), p.30

3. Harrer, Heinrich, *The White Spider* (Rupert Hart-Davis, 1959), p.155

4. ibid., p.164

5. ibid., p.21

6. ibid., p.22

7. ibid., pp.212–213

8. Eliot, T.S., *The Waste Land and Other Poems* (Faber and Faber, 1972), p.37

9. Band, George, *Summit: 150 Years of the Alpine Club* (Harper Collins, 2006), p.168

10. Ellis, Alan, 'Ama Dablam', Summit Post website, www.summitpost. org/ama-dablam/150234 (3 May 2005, accessed 5 December 2019)

11. Rodway, George and Windsor, Jeremy, 'Ama Dablam – 50 Years On', *Alpine Journal* Volume 115 (2010–2011), p.197

12. Kennedy, Michael, 'Ama Dablam', *Alpinist* Issue X (Spring 2005), p.23

13. Ward, Mike, 'The First Ascent', *Alpinist* Issue X (Spring 2005), p.26

14. McNamara, Chris and van Leuven, Chris, *Yosemite Big Walls* (SuperTopo, 2011), p.80

15. Mill, John Stuart, *On Liberty* (Oxford University Press, 2015), p.14

16. Amatt, John, 'Alpamayo, 1966', *Alpine Journal* Volume 72 (1967), p.19 [quoting from Kogan, George and Lenninger, Nicole, *The Ascent of Alpamayo: an account of the Franco-Belgian expedition to the Cordillera Blanca in the High Andes* (George Harrap, 1954)]

17. ibid., p.20

18. ibid., p.18

19. Perrin, Jim, 'Where have all the brave mountaineers gone?', *Telegraph* online, www.telegraph.co.uk/men/active/10721281/Where-have-all-the-brave-mountaineers-gone.html (27 March 2014, accessed 6 January 2020)

20. ibid.

21. Tilman, H.W., *Snow on the Equator,* in *The Seven Mountain-Travel Books* (Diadem Books & Mountaineers Books, 2004), p.43

22. Uren, Allen and Wilson, Mark, *The Mount Aspiring Region: A Guide for Mountaineers* (New Zealand Alpine Club, 2001), p.13

23. Fyfe, T.C., 'The First Complete Ascent of Aorangi', *New Zealand Alpine Journal*, Volume II, Issue 7 (May 1895), p.29 [extracted from an article originally printed in the *Otago Daily Times*, 21 February 1895]

24. Gildea, Damien, *Mountaineering in Antarctica* (Éditions Nevicata, 2010), p.147

ACKNOWLEDGEMENTS

Many have contributed to the creation of this book, in particular the myriad professional and amateur climbers who have been prepared to tie on to the same rope as me. Some of their number are listed at the opening of the book or described within it. I cannot list them all, but I do thank them for their encouragement, their friendship and, importantly, their trust.

Diane Pengelly, wife of my longest-standing climbing partner, did the first full edit of the book, while my two daughters provided copious and thoughtful comments. Mark Seaton, another regular climbing partner over nearly three decades, also read the script, generously allowing me to publish certain details that others might have preferred to remain undisclosed! And the maps and topos were created by yet another of my climbing partners, that man of so many talents, Andy Kirkpatrick. Subsequent revisions, design work, production and marketing have been managed by my publisher Jon Barton and his team at Vertebrate Publishing, including John Coefield, Jane Beagley, Cameron Bonser, Emma Lockley, Jessica McElhattan, Lorna Hargreaves, Rae Helm, Issy Were and Sophie Fletcher. My appreciation and thanks to all of them. As you can tell, it has been very much a team effort.

Any book, but in particular any book of this kind, is made possible only by a support network, built on a clear understanding among loved ones. That network in this case is my family and it is a matriarchy. It has my wife, Rosemary, at its head, followed by our three children. There is somewhat less clarity beyond that, with George the cat I suspect nudging into place just ahead of me. Quite where the goldfish rank is uncertain, but I am quietly confident I am in there ahead of them. Being the matriarch, that is the head of the family, sounds like a privileged position. It really isn't. It means you carry the responsibility for keeping everybody going and the metaphorical world spinning on its axis, while your irresponsible husband casts care aside in foreign parts. There is a genuinely serious point here: what I owe Rosemary is beyond measure. The irony is that she has not read this book and has vowed never to do so. That is part of the understanding.